Can You Wait Just One More Hour?

Can You Wait Just One More Hour?

Single Woman, God Has Not Forgotten You

By
Helen Stubblefield Trowbridge

With
JoAnne Stubblefield Cramberg

PUBLISHING · INC

Tulsa, Oklahoma

Can You Wait Just One More Hour?
(Single Woman, God Has Not Forgotten You)
ISBN 0-9657706-8-0
Copyright © 1998 by
Helen Stubblefield Trowbridge
1037 North Grand Avenue
Suite 101
Covina, California 91724

Published by
PHOS PUBLISHING, INC.
P. O. Box 690447
Tulsa, Oklahoma 74169-0447

Dedication

To My Parents Who Are Now in Glory

Pastor John Milton Stubblefield and
Pastor Lydia Burnett Stubblefield

Daddy was a loving father and a marvelous example of God. He taught the single women in his church that it wasn't a crime to be an "unclaimed blessing." He encouraged young women to wait for God's best.

Mother was my first example of singleness in ministry as she had been a missionary in the Congo and traveled the world in ministry long before she married my father in her late thirties. She again became single after only thirteen years of marriage when my daddy went home to be with the Lord. I marveled at her faith while raising two daughters alone.

What I am today, I owe to the godly lives and prayers of these two wonderful examples of faith.

Contents

Acknowledgements

Tim — My wonderful husband. Next to Jesus you are the best thing that has ever happened to me. Thanks for believing in me, loving and understanding me. I love you, "Hunkster."

JoAnne — My sissy and best friend. Your "Holy Ghost writing" has blessed the Body of Christ. This book could not have come into being without you.

Bishop Carlton D. Pearson — My brother and a mentor in ministry. I have affectionately called you "El Holy-o-Negro." Your example of serving God, as a single man for over twenty years, has been an inspiration to many.

Carman — My brother and loyal friend. We have cried on each other's shoulders and eaten a lot of french fries. Single MAN, God has not forgotten you either!

Oral and Evelyn Roberts — Father and mother in the faith. You taught me to plant, to sow seeds and to wait for the harvest.

Dr. Myles Munroe — My friend for twenty years. "Dr. Purpose" — "Dr. Potential," you are a gift to the Body and because of you — books will be written, songs will be sung. We shall fulfill our purpose, I surely shall fulfil mine.

Dr. Iverna Tompkins — Mother in Israel. You have been my supreme inspiration as a single woman in ministry. I have never heard you complain about God's design for your life. Thank-you.

Dr. Dianne McIntosh — My friend and counselor. Thank-you for helping me on my journey to wholeness. Without you I would have never reached for my highest potential in God. You are the best "Lady Di!"

Sue Riedel — My friend, an anointed intercessor and prophetess. You told me to wait just one more hour. And I'm so glad I did.

Debbie McIntosh — Thanks for encouraging me to wait on my "limo" and not settle for a "Thunderbird"!

Foreword by Carman

Helen Trowbridge, down through the years, has been one of my closest friends. I cannot tell you how many times she has encouraged me and lifted my spirit through her anointed words.

The one thing that impresses me the most about her is that through a long season of singleness, she has maintained a consistent and productive walk with the Lord. She's always been anointed and has never failed to have an appropriate word from God for any difficult situation.

She knows what it is like to feel alone and over-looked, and she also knows what it's like to find God through some of the most adverse personal circum-stances. Her words bring clarity, wisdom, discernment and good old-fashioned common sense to anyone who's open to receive.

I pray that this voice of experience will encourage and strength you as it has done for me over the past seventeen years.

The time for this book is now, and in reading it, your timing is perfect.

Enjoy and be encouraged,

Carman

Nashville, TN

Foreword by Myles Munroe

One of the great challenges of the 21st century is the complex nature of the social pressures confronting the individual. Life is no longer simple. The myriad of choices, alternatives and opportunities are overwhelming.

For the individual who wants to live effectively in this taxing environment, the need for durable principles, precepts, values and morals is critical. It is said that in such a permissive society as reflected in our communities, *"If you don't stand for something, you will fall for anything."*

For the individual who desires healthy, wholesome and helpful relationships, the task is even greater, The unmarried young or not so young woman is one factor that has a difficult challenge. I have counseled hundreds over the past few years who have expressed their frustration, heartache, disillusionment and fears over the prospect of relationships. The need for good, sound, tested and tried advice is necessary to deal with these situations effectively.

In this work, Helen provides practical, potent, scripturally sound advice for the individual facing the trauma of relationship and disappointments. Enriched by her personal experience and testimony as one who survived the ocean of social storms, her insightful, dynamic approach to the subject will help all who are willing to embrace the truth. She offers time-tested answers to age-old questions.

Read on and discover the tremendous life that lies hidden within you that is waiting to be ignited. Read and enjoy this book, which will become a classic for years to come as you learn the value of "waiting just one more hour."

Dr. Myles Munroe
Nassau, Bahamas

Introduction

As a single woman I made a vow to God while waiting on the fulfillment of His promise for a mate. I told God when He blessed me with a husband, I would never forget what it was like to be single. I would always be sensitive to the feelings and needs of people, especially single women. I knew this was important because I had seen so many people who married right out of high school or college. They had never experienced life alone. Most were insensitive and often oblivious to the concerns of singles.

Recently, I read a book written specifically to women, and although it was highly anointed, the chapter to single women lacked compassion and basically did not touch my precious sisters where they were hurting. It said the typical things single women have heard all their lives, "Be thankful that you are single, you can be concerned about the things of God so much more when you are single than if you are married, be content where you are." The author quoted Paul:

> To the unmarried and the widows I say: It is good for them to stay unmarried, as I am.
>
> 1 Corinthians 7:8

> An unmarried woman or virgin is concerned about the Lord's affairs: Her aim is to be devoted to the Lord in both body and spirit. But a married woman is concerned the affairs of this world — how she can please her husband.
>
> 1 Corinthians 7:34

Even though all of that is true, I felt the author did not personally relate to the painful emotions single women experience — whether self-induced or inflicted on them by others. Few really know the heart cry of a single woman — whether never married, divorced or widowed. I know that pain. I did not marry until I had passed by fortieth birthday.

I remember the first time someone made me aware of my singleness. I had never thought of myself as an old maid or an "unclaimed blessing" as my daddy used to say. I was busy in the ministry, traveling around the country with Evangelist Carlton Pearson, who was also single. Most of our team consisted of single men and women who were simply answering the call of God on their lives.

The ministry was fulfilling to me. We ministered to people all over the United States as well as in other parts of the world. After one meeting a young married woman came up to me and said, "You better hurry up and get married, the biological clock is ticking — tick, tick, tick, you'd better hurry."

Another friend said, "Helen, you better hurry up and get married or you are just going to dry up, you are just going to become an old raisin and nobody is going to want you." Years later those words would come back to vex my soul. People can be so sincere — but sincerely wrong!

It is out of my compassion and concern for single women that I write this book. There are so many lovely women in the church who are believing God for their mate. This book carries a prophetic edge that I believe will bring new freedom for you as a single woman of God.

Prophecy is given to edify, exhort and comfort. Most prophecies we hear today are only edification. They are more a word of wisdom or a word of knowledge rather than a prophecy such as, "Behold, my sister, the word of the Lord God is nigh thee, even in thy mouth and the Lord shall open doors and you shall go forth and do this or do that . . . And He is sending your mate." Those words only edify you. With every prophetic word there are conditions, that is the exhortation — the dealings of God in your life. You must go to God — ask what the conditions are in order for the prophecy to come into fruition. In 1 Timothy 1:18, Paul tells us to warfare over the words that have been given to us.

After God has told you to get certain things in your life lined up with His Word, you then need the comfort of the Holy Spirit. The truth will set you free, but first it will make you miserable. Most often we do not want the exhortation. We want to hear that our husband is on the way, but we do not want God to deal in our lives.

The good news is, God has provided the Holy Spirit to be our comfort as we are being operated on. As our flesh is being cut away and we are being made more like God, the Holy Spirit is there to soothe and sustain.

Get ready to be edified, exhorted and then comforted through these words. I am not preaching something I have not lived. I want you to experience the challenging, healing, changing power of God. Single woman, God has not forgotten you.

Chapter 1
You Are Somebody

For we do not have a high priest who is unable to sympathize with our weaknesses, but we have one who has been tempted in every way, just as we are — yet was without sin.

Hebrews 4:15

I heard Oral Roberts interpret this scripture to mean, "Jesus sits where you sit, and He feels what you feel and He knows what you are going through." His interpretation of that Scripture ministered to me so many times as a single young woman. I was trying to serve God and yet hurting because I felt there was something wrong with me because I wasn't married.

Today, my sister, God sits where you sit, He feels what you feel and He does know what you are going through. He has a special place in His heart just for you. You are His baby girl and He loves you more than you can imagine. He will take you up in His arms right now and minister to you if you will let Him.

You are not single because there is something wrong with you. That is a lie of the enemy of your soul. There is nothing wrong with you. At one time or another we have all blamed our appearance for our lack of a mate. You may think your ears stick out, your teeth are crooked or your nose is too big. You may have blamed your less than perfect figure, lack of education, your upbringing, background or past.

1

It's not because you fail to look like a runway model or Miss America. I know a lot of gorgeous women in their thirties who are not married. It baffles me when I see them, a perfect curvaceous size six. They have beautiful teeth, gorgeous eyes, thick hair — perfectly styled, nails manicured and toenails pedicured. They are educated and articulate and well-traveled. I have seen many who are in the ministry alone — not engaged or even dating anyone.

You are not single because you didn't graduate from high school or college. It's not because of the way you were raised or your socioeconomic level. Your dysfunctional family is not to blame. It is not because there are just no single men in your church.

You cannot blame your singleness on your dad because he wouldn't let you marry your high school sweetheart. It is because God has a purpose and perfect timetable for you. We must submit and yield to His purpose and perfect timing and in the process become the ultimate woman of God.

The U.S. Army has adopted as a slogan, "Be all that you can be." I believe that motto is the heart of God for the men and women who are enlisted in the army of the Lord. We need to stop worrying about the things that we think are wrong with us and turn the workmanship over to God. It is time to submit our will to the Father and pray, "God, prepare me for WHO you are preparing for me."

You need to first know how precious you are to God. You must learn to comprehend the depths and the wonders of His love extended toward you. His heart breaks when you cry. He seeks to comfort and minister to you in the nighttime. The word *comfort* means to cause to breathe again.[1] Many times our breath is taken away through grief and pain of loneliness. When the Comforter comes, He causes us to breathe again. He restores our hope.

You were formed by the Creator who also outlined a divine purpose and plan for your life.

> **"For I know the plans I have for you," declares the Lord, "plans to prosper you and not to harm you, plans to give you hope and a future."**
>
> **Jeremiah 29:11**

> **For you created my inmost being; you knit me together in my mother's womb. I praise you because I am fearfully and wonderfully made; your works are wonderful, I know that full well.**

> **My frame was not hidden from you when I was made in the secret place. When I was woven together in the depths of the earth, your eyes saw my unformed body. All the days ordained for me were written in your book before one of them came to be.**
>
> **Psalm 139:13-16**

Billions of people have been born on our planet and yet no one who ever lived has your fingerprints. Your DNA is a genetic fingerprint. DNA testing will identify your unique genetic markers as an individual. It is considered more conclusive identification than even a fingerprint. There is not another person living or dead who possesses the same genetic design God gave you. What other scientific information do you need to know you are unique? You are not a copy of anyone else. Yes,

---

[1] *Strong's Exhaustive Concordance*, "Hebrew and Chaldee Dictionary." Nashville, TN: Crusade Bible Publishers, Inc., p. 77.

you may have your father's eyes, your grandfather's temper and your mother's hips, but you are an original, formed in the womb and birthed into this world for such a time as this.

You are the only one who can be you. No one else has your gifts, your talents or your ability. You are a unique individual, created for a divine purpose. You are single, separate, unique and whole. You are not half a person because you are missing a mate. A mate is given to you, not to complete you but to compliment you for God's purpose. You are not a fraction waiting to be added to, to become a whole. You are whole!

You have been endowed by your Creator with certain gifts no one else possesses. You can touch lives no one else can reach. No one can be better at being you than you. Your place on this earth is a mission, a destiny — not some big mistake in God's scheme of things.

It is your responsibility to find your purpose and to fulfill it with God's help. You must not wait until God sends you a husband to fulfill your purpose. Seek the Father. You have been divinely called to carry out His will on this earth.

God's love for you is a perfect love. His love is unfailing. His love is eternal. His love is faithful. He is not a two-timer. His love is an agape love. His love is unconditional. He does not operate by the world's standard of judging an individual. His opinion of you is not swayed by how you look, how much you weigh, or whether you've got the stuff in the "right places." God wants us to be our best, but He doesn't love us less or devalue us if our teeth are crooked. He loves you unconditionally.

4

God loves us in spite of ourselves, in spite of our frailties, in spite of our weaknesses, and in spite of everything that is in us that is not like Him. He looks beyond our faults and sees our needs. God sees us through the blood of His Son, Jesus.

He sees you as His child and He has a wonderful life planned for you. God watches over you, as you are being transformed into His image and His likeness. He cannot love you any more than He loves you today, and He cannot love you less than He loves you today. No matter what you've done or where you've been, God's love for you never changes.

God knows why you are still single. His purpose will not delay. He is always right on time and right on target. He is not trying to keep something good from you.

> **For the Lord God is a sun and shield; the Lord bestows favor and honor; no good thing does he withhold from those whose walk is blameless.**
>
> **Psalm 84:11**

God is not withholding your blessing of a mate because in the past you fell into sin, messed up or failed Him in some way. It's not because you have already been married and then because of circumstances you are now divorced. God doesn't consider you out of the blessing realm because you got pregnant out of wedlock or decided to have an abortion. God hasn't given up on your future because you have made unwise choices in past relationships.

God has not forgotten His plan for your life because you were once involved in an alternate lifestyle. You are not being punished by God for your past. Yes, there are always consequences for sin, but God does not change His mind about your destiny because you have taken matters of your life into your own hands.

Consider Abraham and Sarah who were given a promise by God for children. They became weary in waiting for God to fulfill His promise and after twelve years took matters into their own hands.

Abraham slept with Hagar, his wife's maid, and she conceived. His first son Ishmael was born from that union. However, God had not forgotten His promise to the couple. When God makes one, He keeps it. He was the original Promise Keeper.

Twenty-five years after the promise, in spite of Abraham's detour, Sarah conceived and Isaac was born — the child of the promise (Genesis 21). Isaac's name means "laughter" and there was great joy in the house when God fulfilled His promise.

In spite of the miracle Abraham still had to deal with the consequences of his moments of unbelief. There was another child to be dealt with and the other woman who became jealous of the child of promise. Abraham had to make some painful decisions regarding the future of his first son.

Sometimes the greatest hindrance to fulfilling our destiny is our inability to forgive ourselves for failing to trust God. It is foolish to beat yourself over the head when the forgiveness was already done at Calvary. Jesus does not have to die again for your every mistake. He already paid the price. You have it available to you. It is simply a matter of accepting what is already available because the price has been paid. Once you repent, God throws your sins into the sea of forgetfulness and never remembers them against you again. He has forgotten. You must forgive yourself. Accept His forgiveness and go on. I once heard Myles Munroe describe the word repent, which comes from two words, *re* and *pent*, as follows: Pent means high — where we get our word penthouse; re means to go back. *Repent* then means to go back to the heights in God.

A young woman once asked an older, godly woman in the church if the devil ever brought up past sins. The woman answered, "Oh, yes, honey, all the time." "Well then," the young woman replied, "what do you do when Satan reminds you of your past?" The woman of faith said, "Well, honey, I send him to the east." "What do you do if he comes back and reminds you again?" the young woman asked. "Well then, I send him to the west because the Scripture says, As far as the east is from the west, so far has he removed our transgressions from us (Psalm 103:12)."

The devil is a liar. He is like the buzzard. The buzzard survives on dead flesh. Often when law enforcement officials are looking for a missing person, they will look for buzzards flying overhead. That is always a sign of a dead body. Buzzards will even dig up shallow graves to feed off rotten flesh.

Like the buzzard, Satan likes to pick at you and remind you of past sins. He likes to dig up things that you consider dead and buried. He brings up the stinking, rotting thing to haunt you again and again. He wants to keep you in condemnation for the mistakes you've made. But once you have been forgiven, the past is just that . . . THE PAST.

> Therefore, there is now no condemnation for
> those who are in Christ Jesus, because through Christ
> Jesus the law of the spirit of life set me free from the
> law of sin and death.
>
> Romans 8:1,2

As Carman said in his song, *Revival in the Land*, "When the devil reminds you of your past, you just remind him of his future." Your future is full of victory. It's Satan's future that is full of defeat.

If Satan were not threatened by your presence, do you think he would bother with you? You are righteous seed and anything you accomplish for the kingdom of God is a direct threat to the kingdom of darkness. Satan knows if you are moving forward in the things of God you are dangerous and he will utilize any method to stop you.

Once you have accepted Christ, you are automatically on Satan's hit list. This should not be a frightening thing for one who is full of the power of God — the Holy Spirit. God created you. You were fearfully and wonderfully made. Then to top it all off, you were given the opportunity to invite Jesus to rule and reign in your life.

He sent the precious Holy Spirit to be your comfort and give you power to overcome every sinister attack of the enemy. With the simple mention of the name Jesus, demons leveled against you have to flee (Philippians 2:9-11). You have the power! You are somebody. You are mighty in God.

God cares for you and wants to give you His very best. He wants to bless His daughter. He longs to give you good gifts. If you ask Him for bread, would He give you a stone (Matthew 7:9-11)? He is your Father and He loves you.

Every good and perfect gift comes from the Father (James 1:17). He delights in blessing His daughters. He desires for you to be fulfilled and happy. You can know today that you are accepted in the Beloved (Ephesians 1:6 KJV).

God has a marvelous plan for your life. Take a new look at yourself and see who you really are. Arise, daughter of the Most High God. Take your place. You are the daughter of the King of the universe and greater is He that is in you than he that is in the world (1 John 4:4).

You are a

> Faith Talker...
>
> Water Walker...
>
> History Maker...
>
> Earth Shaker...
>
> Giant Killer...
>
> Body Healer...
>
> Mountain Mover...
>
> Spirit Soother...
>
> Dead Raiser...
>
> Jesus Praiser...

You are on assignment as Ambassador of the Kingdom of Heaven. You have a crown upon your head and you are dressed in royal garments. You are a crown of splendor in the Lord's hand, a royal diadem in the hand of your God (Isaiah 62).

You have power to call angels to assist you. The forces of heaven are at your access. Take your place. Don't allow any devil, demon, man or negative thought to keep you from your place in the palace of the most High God.

Esther provides us with a great example of God's design for a woman's life. In the natural, she had some roadblocks to overcome. She was a Jewess, a minority, and had been ordered by her guardian to keep it a secret. She was an orphan. It was her natural beauty that first captured the attention of the men in the service of the king.

Strange as it may seem in light of our doctrine and religious morals of today, Esther was predestined by God to be a second wife.

Now don't use this example as an excuse to walk outside of God's will for your life. You see, God had a higher plan than simply a mate for Esther. Her mate was chosen by God, and He had a divine purpose in that union. That marriage was God's design for the deliverance of His people.

After a year of beauty treatments and preparation, Esther was prepared to go before the king. She understood her place. When the issue went beyond her natural capabilities, she knew to seek wisdom and direction from God through prayer and fasting. Esther knew the personal power she possessed, but it did not overshadow her need for the power of God. She was a woman of purpose.

Women sometimes fail to recognize their personal power, and those who do know often misuse it. Jezebel used her feminine wiles to control and

manipulate. She became food for dogs: Purina — Alpo
. . . . That is an example of power gone wrong.

It is time to be honest with ourselves. We must first
recognize our power — both personal and spiritual —
then evaluate how we are using it. Learn to speak to
yourself. Tell yourself the truth. Tell yourself who you
are in God. Have God-esteem. Have good self-esteem.
When His Spirit is your driving force, you will have no
need to control and manipulate situations. God will be
in control. No matter what your circumstances — you
are somebody. You are special. You are unique.

One of the greatest attacks against single women
comes in the form of deadly negative emotions. We
often allow them to control us and the low self-esteem
entraps us. If the enemy can keep us captive (having
the appearance of freedom, but being in bondage to
something), he can literally keep us from being in the
right place at the right time. We can be so caught up in
our own neediness that we miss an opportunity God
has prepared.

Older singles are particularly at risk when it comes
to giving in to a spirit of gloom, despair and agony —
deep, dark depression, excessive misery. As each birthday passes we tend to become more anxious and
convinced God has forgotten us.

Many single women are on the verge of suicide.
They have worked to perfect themselves. Countless trips
to the gym have toned and reduced them. Cosmetic
surgery has lifted and enhanced every physical feature.
Facials, manicures and pedicures have given a polished
appearance. Thousands of dollars have been spent on
cosmetics and clothes to look good.

Education and knowledge of the world have been pursued. Making certain they have done everything in their power to be the kind of woman a man would want, they have read at least a dozen books on relationships and how to get a man. Dr. Love has told them how to have successful relationships, and how to keep that man once you get him.

The best relationship manual you will ever find is the Word of God. Read it to discover God's great plan and purpose for your life. You are special. You are unique. But, becoming all you can be will require change. Some of your flesh will have to die. Many of your plans and dreams will have to be surrendered to God — but there is great hope.

Do you really want to change? Have you already tried everything you know? God loves you just the way you are, but He wants to maximize your potential. He wants you to be the best to fulfill the purpose of His call on your life. Are you ready to allow God to change you? Will you submit to the skillful hands of His spiritual surgery for your life?

Surgery is never easy, but the Holy Spirit will be your comfort. If you are really ready to see your potential in God, then He is waiting and ready to maximize your potential. You are a woman designed and chosen by God for such a time as this. You are a woman full of purpose with a divine destiny.

Chapter 2
Do You Want to Get Well?

Some time later, Jesus went up to Jerusalem for a feast of the Jews. Now there is in Jerusalem near the Sheep Gate a pool, which in Aramaic is called Bethesda and which is surrounded by five covered colonnades [porches]. Here a great number of disabled people used to lie — the blind, the lame, the paralyzed. One who was there had been an invalid for thirty-eight years. When Jesus saw him lying there and learned that he had been in this condition for a long time, he asked him, "Do you want to get well?"

John 5:1-6

Many single women desire a husband and they are not well — not whole. They keep thinking that a man will complete them. Two halves in a relationship do not make a whole. Two whole people coming together make a whole marriage. If you marry and you are not well, if you are not whole, you will be more miserable than when you were single.

I once heard a young woman say, "If I hadn't gotten married, I would have never dealt with some issues in my life." That was a sad statement. She and her husband have had tremendous problems in their marriage because neither of them worked on becoming whole as single people. Marriage will be much happier for you and your spouse, if while you are single, you both work on becoming whole.

Several years before I married, I realized that even as a Spirit-filled Christian, ordained into the ministry, I was not well. I had some emotional issues I had refused to face as I was on a breakneck schedule to minister to the world. I was saved, Spirit-filled and trying to live holy as I perceived from the Scriptures, but I was not happy.

My relationships had problems, I was somewhat codependent and a people pleaser. I was what you wanted me to be when I was with you, and what the other person wanted me to be when I was with them. This emotional instability resulted from unresolved issues in my life. I was not whole. I was a double-minded person, unstable in many of my ways, and definitely in the area of relationships.

Thank God for His precious Holy Spirit and godly counsel. I went to God and also to a Christian counselor and confessed my sin. Facing the fact that I had wanted to please people more than God was painful for me. In a sense I was an idolater. I placed man's opinion of me above God's opinion of me, and anything that takes precedence over God in your life is an idol.

I wanted and needed the approval of people more than I wanted God's approval. When I didn't get the approval of man, I would go into depression for days. If someone didn't like me or I thought they didn't like me, I would retreat. God often whispered to me, "Something is wrong inside of you, Helen." Something was wrong. I finally decided to allow God to make me whole no matter how painful the process. I was already miserable. How much more miserable could I be? I needed a change in my life. I had to get well.

Do you have to desire to get well? It is a choice. God does not beat you over the head with your imperfections, but He often sheds His light on the darkened corners of your life. He wants these things exposed so you will surrender them to Him for healing. Many times when the same issue in life confronts you again and again, it is simply God's attempt to get your attention about something that needs healing.

Becoming whole does not come through just going to the altar and praying. It doesn't come just by fasting and praying, although both of these are important in your search for wholeness.

One single woman I know fasts and prays continually. She will stay in her room and you can hear her crying out to God. But this same woman has not worked for over twenty years. She is on mental disability with government assistance and cannot work. All of her fasting and praying has not made her whole. I wonder in her prayer time, is she ever listening? The Bible says the effectual fervent prayer of the righteous availeth much (James 5:16 KJV).

If your prayers are not being answered, you need to go back to God and make sure you are in obedience to what He told you. Wholeness comes after you have prayed and fasted and then walked out what God said to you. Wholeness requires radical obedience. Many fast and pray, all the while failing to obey the last directive God gave them.

A preacher who was publicly exposed because of a major sin in his life had said repeatedly he didn't believe in Christian counselors — everything could be handled at the altar. He was a man who preached a lot about the power of the Holy Ghost. If his statements were true, then in his own life, he could have gotten his deliverance at the altar. Obviously, he had not been delivered, because the fruit of his life eventually publicly exposed some very private issues.

If you have not listened and learned to allow God's dealings, then you probably do need a Christian counselor. Sometimes our past pain is so pronounced we cannot hear the voice of the Lord. The pathway to wholeness is a strenuous journey. Many who know they have a problem would rather continue to suffer than to deal with the issues before God.

I am not ashamed to say that I submitted myself to intense counseling for a six-week period. I still talk to my counselor from time to time. I had to shut out work, cease all other activities and focus on what God wanted to do in me.

Today as I deal with issues I can't handle on my own, I seek help in discerning myself. The Word reminds me to, "Confess your faults one to another that you might be healed" (James 5:16).

God now often uses my husband to counsel me in understanding my personal weaknesses. God even uses him to convict me and help me line up in obedience to God.

In the fifth chapter of John, Jesus came to the pool of Bethesda where He observed a large group of sick people. Pretend for a moment that all of these people were single women, sitting around, waiting and wanting to get whole. They were looking for their miracle. They were in the right place at the right time, but the majority were not receiving their healing.

Most of them probably thought — "Well, she got her miracle. When will it be my turn? What about me?" The people in this passage of Scripture all believed that when an angel stirred the waters, the first person into the water would be made whole.

There are many people in the church who desire wholeness. They are sitting around the waters of the Spirit waiting for God to touch them. What they do not realize is that God is within them. He is just wanting for them to stir up the waters in their own lives and receive the wholeness He has for them.

The people lying around the pool had infirmities that kept them from becoming whole. The Scripture tells us that there were many sick people lying there by that pool. They were disabled. The word *disabled* means to make motionless or powerless by damage or injury, to be crippled or embolized or incapacitated.[1] Another dictionary uses impotent for one of the definitions. Impotency keeps you from reproducing. When you are impotent you have no fruit in your life. You lack strength and vigor. You are weak, powerless and ineffectual.

The Word says some there at the pool were blind. I'll be painfully honest, I was blind, but praise God, now I see. I've never been blind to the weaknesses of those around me. I can discern everybody else. I can tell everyone else what their problem is, I always have knowledge about what is wrong with everyone else. But when it comes to me, to look at myself in the mirror and recognize my own weaknesses and frailties — that is another story. I had to go to God and say, "Open my

---

[1] *Webster's II New Riverside University Dictionary*, p. 381.

blinded eyes, let me see me. Let me see the good in me, but also show me the bad in me, so I can begin to change." I wanted to bring my body under subjection, to say no to my flesh and to this sinful nature.

I had never recognized I had a temper. I was blind to the fact I often raised my voice and pointed my finger in a discussion. I had to allow God to remove the scales from my eyes and allow me to see myself once and for all — the good, the bad and the ugly. Proverbs 16:32 says, "Better a patient man than a warrior, a man who controls his temper than one who takes [captures] a city." We have to capture ourselves first before we can take away cities. We must surrender.

When you surrender, God will open your eyes and show you the truth. We are always trying to get the speck out of another's eye when we have a log in our own eye (Matthew 7:3).

The Bible says the lame were there by the pool. These people were crippled in their walk. A lot of single women are crippled in their walk. They are hurt in one or more of their limbs so that walking or moving is easily hampered. This lameness is marked by pain or rigidness. The are unable to walk holy. They have succumbed to sexual promiscuity thinking that the sexual love of a man will help.

Sexual relationships have become a substitute for what they really want which is a happy, healthy home. They think they will get the man by giving him what he wants, when in reality, he usually leaves them. They go limping from one bad relationship to another unable to walk in true holiness because they are looking for love in all the wrong places. Many other things can cause you to limp. Addictions, habits, hobbies, and wrong thinking hinder our walk and, women, we can have an attitude — or "tude" as some call it. Your bad attitude hinders your walk. Carrying all of your problems yourself can keep you from walking on that straight and narrow path God has for you.

There are others who are completely *paralyzed* — unable to move. They have allowed the fears of life to paralyze them. They've been in bad relationships or perhaps were hurt by family members. Circumstances have caused them to be full of fear and unable to move in the things of God. The Word says that God has not given us a spirit of fear, but of power and of love and of a sound mind (2 Timothy 1:7).

Here at the pool were the impotent, disabled, blind, lame and paralyzed. They were unable to get into the water, laying on those five porches. The porches are things that hinder our wholeness. They represent different levels of our unhealthy state. Yes, we are saved. We go to church and are trusting God on some level to deliver us, but we are laying on one of the porches and cannot get to the water for healing.

Jesus came on the scene and asked the man, "Do you want to get well?" The man gave Jesus his excuse for not receiving his healing.

> **"Sir," the invalid replied, "I have no one to help me into the pool when the water is stirred. While I am trying to get in, someone else goes down ahead of me." Then Jesus said to him, "Get up! Pick up your mat and walk." At once the man was cured; he picked up his mat and walked.**
>
> **John 5:7-9**

These disabled people were lying on five porches. They were just waiting to be healed. The Lord began to show me the porches in my own life and how I needed to get off of the porch in order to be made whole. I wasn't just on one porch, but I had a number of porches hindering my wholeness.

Compromise

The first porch I recognized was the porch of compromise. I grew up in a strict Pentecostal family where everything was a sin. We didn't go bowling, we didn't play cards, we didn't roller skate, ice skate or even play marbles — "Marble not." We didn't do anything that could or would keep us from the will of God.

Today the Church has gone to the opposite end of the spectrum. Some have completely discarded the true tenants of holiness. Saints are tipping, dipping, sipping and compromising in their lives. Some Christian single women I know are involved in immorality. And if they are not involved in that, there are other compromises in their lives. God says He is coming for a Church without a spot or wrinkle, but washed in the blood of the Lamb (Ephesians 5:27).

The Lord wants us to live holy. None of us are perfect and I never would pretend to be. But there is a great difference in living in sin and committing sin. We all sin, but to make the choice to live in sin is a different story.

Sometimes we are not honest on our jobs. We take office supplies belonging to the company home for personal use. We call in sick when we just want to clean the house or be lazy for a day. We take long lunch hours and make long distance phone calls at the company's expense.

Some people pirate computer programs and run countless personal copies on the company machine. Where do you think the testimony goes when you act like every other ungodly person? You are stealing from your employer. You are compromising the Christian witness and your walk of holiness when you misuse your position for personal gain.

When we are saved we are to take on the character of Jesus. If we are acting like Satan — lying, cheating, stealing — then we can no longer say God is in us.

These are only a few examples of how a Christian can compromise. There are countless others, some I have been guilty of and others I have seen in the Body of Christ. I am certain God is sick of compromise. Attitudes must die. Motives and intents of our hearts must be purified and cleansed.

Compromising is being lukewarm. The Lord said, "I'd rather have you hot or cold because if you're lukewarm, I'll spew you out of My mouth" (Revelation 3:15,16).

God is getting out His spiritual Roto-Rooter and dealing with our fleshly lives. He is cleaning house. It's time to get off the porch of compromise. If there is any compromise in your life right now, I pray in the name of Jesus that you will repent and change your mind. Ask the Lord to deliver you from a spirit of compromise. The Lord will do His part, but you must do yours. Make the right choices that lead to holiness in your life.

Blame

The second porch the Lord showed me was the porch of blame. This was the porch where the man was lying in our passage. When Jesus asked the man if he wanted to get well, he didn't say yes. Instead he said, "I don't have anybody to help me get in the pool." It was another's fault the man had not gotten into the healing stream.

We have the tendency to blame others for where we are in our lives. I don't believe there is anything worse than a child being sexually molested. It is a violation that paralyzes many people throughout their lives. You may have been molested as a child and have never been able to overcome that issue in your life. Now is the time to get off that porch and receive your healing.

We are not responsible for what others do to us. We are, however, responsible to God for our responses. When we get to heaven and God speaks to us concerning things in our lives, we can't say we didn't live up to our spiritual potential because Uncle Johnny did this, or our stepfather did that. We are responsible for our own actions when it comes to responding to negative situations. Stop blaming someone else. Forgive and let God deal with the response. It's all about — you and your relationship with God.

At one point while in ministry, my sister and I worked in the same organization. A woman on the ministry staff had been talking about my sister and it made me mad. In fact I was furious with her. The woman did not know it, but I literally hated her. My sister is sweet and kind and had not done anything to the woman.

22

My sister had been employed by the ministry and this woman had received a promotion when my sister filled her old position. Even though the woman received a promotion with a higher salary, in reality she wanted the old position because it was a bit more prestigious in her opinion. She was undermining my sister with her derogatory comments, talking to other people in the office who would then come and tell me.

One day I was sitting in my office preparing to go away and minister for the weekend in a church where there had never been a woman in their pulpit or a white minister either. I was coming up against some strong religious prejudices. I was white and I was a woman. I was going there to bring a message of reconciliation and to stir the healing waters.

God had opened this door and I knew I would need His help to walk in humility. It was an awesome and holy opportunity. As I was praying for the anointing and wisdom and for the right word, the Lord spoke clearly to my heart. He warned me He would close this door to ministry if I didn't go to this lady who had been talking and apologize.

Of course I whined, "God, why should I go and apologize to that lady? She is the one who has gossiped. She is the one who should be apologizing." The Lord said so clearly to me, "Helen, you are not responsible for what she has done, but you are responsible for your attitude and the bitterness that is in your heart."

I ran to the lady and repented. I asked her to forgive me for harboring bitterness against her. I was set free and she was too. This lady and I are still good friends. (Several years later she left that ministry and went to work for another ministry that has a policy of firing any employee who is caught talking about another employee.)

She called me after she started working there and thanked me for coming to her several years ago. She said, "Helen, that delivered me." So you see we were both delivered.

If a hypocrite is standing between you and God, they are closer to God than you are. You are responsible for you. You have to make the decision to forgive.

Forgiving is not forgetting. It is very difficult to forget a terrible deed that has been done to you, but you can forgive. Forgiveness is a process. We make the decision to forgive and then God starts the healing process. You will know that the process is complete when you can remember the incident and pray for the person to be blessed who perpetrated the deed against you. When you can be happy that they are blessed and rejoice for them, you are truly healed.

Remember this, Job's complete restoration came after he prayed for His friends (Job 42:10). Double . . . Double . . . Double blessings came upon him after he prayed. When you can pray for those who have abused you, healing flows.

God, help us get off the porch of *blame*. Ask for God's forgiveness just now if you have been hanging out on this porch. Pray this prayer with me, "Forgive me, God, for not taking responsibility for my own sins and for blaming others. Help me to forgive those who have wounded me in the past and even those who are wounding me right now. Forgive them, God, as You have forgiven me, for I realize that I cannot be forgiven unless I first forgive. Thank You for setting me free."

Bitterness and Jealousy

The next porch the Lord showed me was the porch of *bitterness and jealousy*. I have to be very honest with you, this was one of my favorite hangouts. I was jealous of other women, particularly married women. I would look at them and wonder why they had a husband and I did not. I was just as cute or as smart or as nice as they were, yet I was alone. When I saw married couples hold hands, I was resentful. Many times in church settings I would be the only single person. It was very painful. I was bitter against people and bitter against God. God told me, "Helen, I can't bless you with a husband if you have a spirit of jealousy."

He told me what to do, and I obeyed. I began to plant into married couples' lives. When I heard they were having an anniversary, I would give the husband money to take his wife out for dinner. I began planting seeds and being happy that others were happily married. I was planting seeds in good soil, believing that someday I would have an anniversary of my own. I've just passed my third. Praise God.

I see women in the church whose physical appearance has actually changed due to bitterness. They have become wrinkled and look older than they really are because of bitterness. The Bible says that a life full of envy and jealousy rots the bones (Proverbs 14:30). Diseases can more easily attack people who are full of these attitudes.

The Lord continued to deal with my jealousy. There was a woman in the church I did not like. She had some "big" sin in her life and yet she was a part of the praise and worship team. I didn't think the pastor should let her sing, but he did anyway. When she would get up to sing, I would put my head down like I was praying or looking for some great Scripture in my Bible. I call it acting "deep." It didn't matter to me how anointed her gift was, she wasn't living right. It wasn't by gossips that I knew she wasn't living holy, she told me herself.

I decided to go to God about her. I self-righteously got down on my knees and said in my prayer voice, "Lord, I want to talk to You about Mary (not her real name). I just rebuke that fornicating spirit in Jesus' name." The Lord spoke back to me, "Shut up, Helen, I don't want you talking to me about Mary. I want to talk to you about YOU."

I was shocked, "What do You mean, Lord, I'm not lying and I'm not fornicating. I'm living holy." The Lord said, "You are doing something much worse. First of all, Helen, Mary is a size three. (I'm not a size three, I have never been a size three except for when I was three years old.) Mary has beautiful skin, she has never had a zit (pimple). Mary has shiny thick hair that sways in the wind. When Mary walks down the street all the men look at her." If I had been walking with Mary, I might well have been a bush. No one was looking at me.

By the time the Lord finished His dialogue, I recognized I was much worse off than Mary. No, I wasn't doing what she was doing but I was worse — I was self-righteous. I had exalted myself over her. I was full of jealousy. I immediately repented. I asked God to forgive me. I didn't need to ask Mary for forgiveness because she did not know how I had been feeling, but I did hug her and love her — and this time I really meant it. It is a great thing to be free of jealousy and bitterness. You need to know this, Mary hasn't changed, but I have.

Jealousy and bitterness eat away at you. They make you miserable. Today I am free. It is wonderful to be free. When I see women who are more attractive than me, I do not experience deadly negative emotions. When I see women much thinner than myself with perfect figures, I'm glad someone can wear those size 3's, 5's and 6's that fill the stores. God bless 'em.

If you are bitter at God, ask Him to deliver you. You will experience freedom such as you have never known. Come off the porch of bitterness and jealousy, you will be the happiest you have ever been in your life.

Self-Pity

The fourth porch is the porch of *self-pity*. So many young women are in this "poor pitiful me" state. I'm not married — poor me. I'm not educated — poor me. I'm struggling with the past — poor me. I don't have enough money — poor me.

Many really enjoy feeling sorry for themselves because they get attention that way. They send out invitations to their pity party. God told me to quit feeling sorry for myself, that I wasn't the only one going through something difficult. He told me I wasn't the only lonely woman in the world. He told me I wasn't the only young woman trying to live right and waiting for the right man to come into my life. He said, "Helen, get off of the porch of *self-pity*. I cannot use you if you are going to keep feeling sorry for yourself." My own words kept me in a prison.

Life and death are in the power of the tongue (Proverbs 18:21). When you speak negatively about yourself, you feed that emotion. The more you say you are unwanted, the more unwanted you will feel. The more you tell yourself you are ugly, the more ugly you become. The more lonely you say you are, the more alone you will feel. Quit feeding those deadly negative emotions with your own words.

> **Casting down imaginations, and every high thing that exalteth itself against the knowledge of God, and bringing into captivity every thought to the obedience of Christ.**
>
> **2 Corinthians 10:5 KJV**

I had to get off the porch and realize that there were a lot of other women who were hurting. Some of their pain was worse than mine. I invited five or six women over on Valentine's Day. At each of their places I had a love note from Jesus telling them how special they were. There was a single parent there, a young woman whose husband had abused her and she was separated and several other young women who had never been married. I had gone to Marshall's and bought them each a little gift — earrings, a necklace or bracelet. Something just to let them know they were loved.

You are not the only one hurting today. Yes, maybe all of your close friends have married, but it doesn't mean that they are all hilariously happy. And there are plenty more single women, some older than you, some who have been through more painful circumstances than you. Get out of yourself and out of your self-pity. Reach out to them and God will bless you.

Several years ago I was dating a nice young man in our church. We had a good relationship, but he couldn't make a commitment to marry me. When we broke up, I looked at him in the face and I said, "I'm going to get married, I have a promise from God. God never told me it was you I would marry. So you go your way, because I will be getting married and you will see me walk down the aisle with someone."

In that moment of pain, I had to speak what I knew to be the truth. And now let the weak say I am strong, let the poor say I am rich, let the lonely say I have friends and God sets the lonely in families. Yes, I was hurt, but I had a promise from God and I was not going to feel sorry for myself because I didn't have anyone to date. I wasn't going to feel sorry for myself because this man couldn't make a commitment. It wasn't my fault he couldn't commit. God had someone better for me and I couldn't allow a spirit of self-pity to take over.

Don't fall into the devil's trap of self-pity. When you are feeling sorry for yourself, you carry an aura around you. It is a spirit that most people will not want to be around. No one wants to associate with someone who is *always* in need of encouragement.

Lost Faith

The fifth porch is the saddest of all the porches because it is the porch of *lost faith*. Not long ago I spoke with a young woman in her mid-forties. She has never married and desperately desires to be. She has given up. She has lost her faith and hope. She knew God could, but she no longer believed He would.

The Word tells us that which is not of faith is sin (Romans 14:23). Many are living in sin because they have lost their faith. They no longer believe God really cares about their personal life.

As long as you stay in that state, you literally tie God's hands. For "do-nothings," God does nothing. You have to step out in faith and believe that in spite of your present circumstances, God will come through for you.

I remember when Pastor Carlton Pearson got married, all of a sudden everyone was feeling sorry for me. We had been the only two singles left on the ministry staff. The Sunday after he married, I got up in front of the congregation and said, "Don't feel sorry for me, the Lord has made me a promise that I am getting married. I may be old. If I'm in a wheelchair, you may have to roll me down the aisle, but you will see me come down this aisle in marriage, because I have a promise from God" (Jeremiah 29:11).

You have to hope, believe and trust God despite the circumstances. "Blessed is she who has believed that what the Lord has said to her will be accomplished!" (Luke 1:45). I was blessed because I believed God would come through for me, even though at the time of that positive confession I didn't even have a steady boyfriend.

Your faith puts God in motion on your behalf. He is searching for people to bless. Pray, God help me to come off the porch of lost faith, hopelessness and despair. Help me learn to trust You in spite of the circumstances.

I knew a woman who was in her forties. I was in her church ministering. Susan had not really dated in years, but she had been faithful to God and to the ministry in her local church. It seemed like everyone else was married — at times self-pity would attach itself to her. God told me to tell her publicly He was about to bless her. She had watched other people being blessed and it was her turn. I asked the Lord why I had to tell her this publicly, couldn't I just tell her in private? The Lord said, "All the people have to hear this."

Obediently, I told her God was going to bless her with a husband within one year. She was a little mad at me for telling her that publicly, she was embarrassed because I even shared what God had revealed about how she was feeling on the inside. She did, however, trust the word of the Lord.

A few months later a man in the church began to take her out as a friend. I prophesied to her in January and eleven months later I was a part of her wedding ceremony. God helped her to get off the porch of self-pity when He gave her a personal word. God has a word for you too, but you must have faith that He is moving even when you cannot see or feel Him.

If you recognize you are on one of those porches or God has revealed something in your life that needs changing, pray this prayer with me: "Dear Jesus, forgive me for my sins, forgive me for compromising, for allowing jealousy and bitterness in my life. Forgive me for placing blame on others, for feeling sorry for myself, for walking in fear, doubt and unbelief. Cleanse me and sanctify me now. Purify my heart, God. I long to be more like You. Lord, I desire to get well."

If you really meant that prayer, God will begin to work on you. Many of us pray, "Lord have Your way," but when He starts having His way in our lives, we refuse to submit, because dying to our flesh is a painful process. When He starts His process of transformation, if you balk, He will not persist. But if you say yes, even

Chapter 3
I Haven't Got Time for the Pain

Pain in our life is an indication that something is wrong. We have often treated the symptoms but have not gotten to the root issues. If the root is dug out and destroyed, the pain is gone.

You could give yourself an aspirin to get rid of a headache momentarily, but sooner or later the headache will return if you have not dealt with the reason for the pain. Many people go from one symptom to another in their lives, trying to deal with the pain themselves instead of going to the Father.

> **Casting the whole of your care** (your pain) **[all your anxieties, all your worries, all your concerns, once and for all] on Him, for He cares for you affectionately and cares about you watchfully.**
>
> **1 Peter 5:7 AMP**

We have learned to cope with most pain. We pray, but if the pain continues, we do something about it. We run to the local drugstore where we can find something for almost every minor ailment from heartburn to a headache. The medication eases the pain momentarily but none of them heal the pain source. They don't go to the root of the problem. They just help cover the symptoms. These medications only mask the problem with temporary relief.

Just because you are saved doesn't mean everything is right in your life. Many committed Christians have serious root issues in their lives. When you get saved, your spirit gets saved, your flesh doesn't get saved. Your flesh will not go to heaven, but it can keep your spirit from heaven. That is one reason Paul said, "I die daily" (1 Corinthians 15:31). "I beat my body and make it my slave" (1 Corinthians 9:27). The Bible reminds us to walk in the Spirit so we will not fulfill the lusts of the flesh (Galatians 5:16).

Many years ago, we hired an anointed man to minister to our youth. He was a powerful man in his gifts. He could preach you out of your seat and could pray like a whirlwind. Before he was saved, he had been a pimp. He had gotten saved while in prison. We first hired him to be the janitor and he did a great job. He had such rapport with the young people that he was hired to be the youth pastor a year later.

For the first year he did a great job with the youth. But telltale signs of a root issue in his life began to surface. I started noticing that he came to church almost every Sunday with new clothes and his wife only had about four or five dresses. He would have new snake shoes and a new suit and his wife would be wearing the same clothes. His children were shabbily dressed but he was always sharp. That was the spirit of a pimp, one who takes care of himself first. That is the epitome of a selfish person.

A few months later, he started physically abusing his wife and then fell into sin with one of the teenage girls in the youth department. He fathered a child with her. It wasn't that he had not been saved. He was gifted of the Holy Ghost. But he had a root issue in his life that

34

had never been dealt with. Even though he had gotten saved, he still had the symptoms of a pimp. He had never asked God to show him the root issues in his life. You see, people are pimps for a reason. It's not because they are bad or evil. It is because they have a root in their life that they have never dealt with and have never let Dr. Jesus heal.

That is why it is critical to the Body of Christ that you deal with your root issues. Why do you react the way you do when someone talks about you? Why do you need to control people? Why do you run and hide? What are your issues? What is the X factor in your life? What is the root? Is it low self-esteem? Is it insecurity? Whatever it is, Jesus wants to show you. He wants to deliver you and fill that void in your life with Himself and His precious Holy Spirit. You must be willing to deal with your issues. Don't be like the man at the pool who sat there ill for thirty-eight years. Get your deliverance today. Let the Lord deal with your pain. He will set you free.

I searched the Scriptures for biblical examples of dealing with pain. The technology of today is advanced, but the manner of coping then was much as it is today. Moses dealt with the pain of injustice when he saw a man killing another. He couldn't deal with that pain, so he killed the man. Then he couldn't deal with his sin so he went into hiding for forty years in the desert. He retreated from the pain. I wonder what would have happened had Moses gone to God when he first saw this injustice. It might have changed the entire course of history for the Israelites.

Sarah dealt with the pain of feeling totally useless and barren by taking matters into her own hands. She didn't allow God to be in control. A controlling spirit was Sarah's pain reliever. In the Garden of Gethsemane the disciples couldn't face the fact that Jesus was soon to leave them. They slept to avoid the pain. Peter dealt with the pain by being violent, cutting of the soldier's ear.

Judas dealt with his pain of betraying Jesus. He had listened to the teachings of Jesus and probably thought he would help by pushing Jesus to establish His earthly kingdom. Surely Jesus would deliver Himself and His reign could begin. But it didn't happen that way and instead of crying out for forgiveness, Judas's pain reliever was to commit suicide.

When faced with life's pain, we have two choices — to seek healing and restoration through God, or to seek the solution in ourselves. When we seek the solution in ourselves we make destructive decisions.

Those people who seek solutions in themselves often become workaholics. They seek gratification and acceptance from what they do. Sometimes they become expert controllers, thinking if they are in control, everything will be all right.

Others become rebels like many of our teenagers today. They rebel to get attention. The gangs are a counterfeit family. They have pain in their real family or the intense pain of no family at all, so they create one of their own.

Sometimes chronic victimization offers an escape from the real truth in the depths of a person's soul. Some are repeatedly mistreated, always hurt or wounded. Many never accept the responsibility for climbing out of the hog-pen of their circumstances. They prefer to sit in the mud, wallow in it, and seek sympathy for their plight.

For more than twenty years I have worked in the ministry. I have watched as Christians attempted to deal with pain instead of taking the cure — giving them to Jesus. We search for pain relievers and instead of spelling relief J-E-S-U-S, we go to the doctor for medication that will keep us in a zombie state. Yes, Christians do use drugs to mask their pain. If they are prescribed by a doctor we somehow legitimize their use. I have seen some even turn to alcohol to numb the pain.

Eating is one of the greatest pain relievers. It is a socially acceptable comfort fix — and there is a fast-food crack house on every corner. Many obese people are full of pain and they find solace in the refrigerator. At age seven, after my father died I wouldn't eat for two months. The doctor gave me pills to increase my appetite. I began to find solace in food, instead of finding solace in the Father. He said He would be a father to the fatherless (Psalm 68:5).

I have a dear friend who was a beautiful girl and tragically, she was raped. After that devastating rape, she began to eat and eat and ballooned to over 300 pounds. She thought in the back of her mind that the food would take the pain away and also it would keep anyone else from wanting to abuse her.

Shopping can numb the pain. There is even a slogan for it, "When the going gets tough, the tough go shopping." I understand this. I have purchased things I will never use. Many have maxed out their MasterCard to mask their pain. Millions of dollars did not heal Princess Diana's painful marriage. Another more gorgeous gown or piece of jewelry would not take away the pain of an unfaithful husband.

People use stimulants to make them forget their pain. They use arousal relievers — things which excite and stir them up. Sexual immorality such as promiscuity, pornography, or lusting all temporarily ease the pain. A one-night stand is just that, but many do it to numb the pain of not feeling loved. Unfortunately, as with most pain relievers, there can be harmful and even deadly side effects.

Some are now calling the physic hotlines. They want someone to tell them they are going to meet a tall, dark, handsome stranger and money is coming their way. If Dionne Warwick doesn't even know "The way to San Jose," how can she help you with your life? Too bad she wasn't able to prophesy that her own network would go bankrupt.

Christians should not involve themselves with the physic hotlines, because doing so opens the door to spirits of darkness. Physic hotlines excite people and take the pain away just for a little while. They offer false hope and false promises that they cannot bring to pass.

Many are addicted to exercise. Exercise is good for us all, but exercising can become an addiction. Some people run miles a day to relieve the pain in their lives. They think if they stay in shape they will be loved and accepted. Many are actually running from the truth.

I know a man who was unfaithful to his wife most of their married life. He was an avid exerciser. He did it in the rain, sleet or snow. It was his way of escape. He refused to deal with himself and his adulterous ways. He was addicted to exercise because in some small way, it made him feel better about himself. He thought if he looked good on the outside, if he was in shape, that meant to the onlookers that he was o.k. — a good person, a great guy.

Gambling and risk taking have become pain relievers. Most Christians wouldn't think about going to Las Vegas to gamble, but every new network marketing product that comes out, they are in it. I know someone who was into selling crosses, then Amway, then Meadowfresh, then some kind of mineral drink. Next it was Herbal Life, some water softener and Mellaluca. You name it and he got into it. His desire was to be rich, thinking that if he became rich, he would be accepted. The root of his illness was low self-esteem. He needed healing, not another network marketing scheme.

The fantasy world offers an escape from pain. Comic books, romance novels, action hero movies — anything that takes one out of the real world. We have a "Take me away Calgon" mentality. Addiction to movies and videos provides an escape. Escape from your real world comes by living through the happiness and sadness of others. All of these aren't bad in themselves, but to be addicted is the fantasy life.

It's amazing as I travel on planes how many people are going into another world by reading books. Most of the books I see are fiction, fantasy and spy novels. Anything that keeps people from thinking about the issues in their lives. They haven't got time for the pain. But there is a warning call out to us today. We must have time for the pain. Allow God to show you the disease in your soul. We need healing.

The soap opera addiction makes your pain seem small. No one's life is as bad as the lying, cheating, murdering, manipulating, beautiful soap star. She has been demon possessed, had amnesia, seven husbands, three abortions, a disfiguring car accident and a prison sentence. She's been an alcoholic and gone to drug rehab. Her son murdered his wife. One of her husbands gave her a sexually transmitted disease and one of her daughters was fathered by a doctor in town to whom she was never married. In comparison our lives are blessed. The entertainment industry is flourishing and literally billions of dollars are being spent to help people escape from the pain in their lives.

The latest escape has been provided by technology. It is computers and computer games. People are spending hours on their computers to keep from dealing with the issues in their lives. They can talk to complete strangers in chat-rooms and avoid talking to God.

You need to check your motives and intentions. Are you using life's pleasures in excess to avoid issues? What kind of pain relievers are you using? Jesus wants to be your complete comfort. Jesus doesn't just deal with the symptoms, He gets to the root of the issue.

He provided our greatest example of someone who dealt with His own pain. The Bible says they hurled their insults at Him and they mistreated Him and He turned Himself over to the One who judges justly (1 Peter 2:23).

No one person or thing can meet all of your needs. Only Jesus can do that. He is the only One who can satisfy your soul.

The Spirit of the Sovereign Lord is on me,
because the Lord has anointed me to preach good

news to the poor. He has sent me to bind up the brokenhearted, to proclaim freedom for the captives and release from darkness for the prisoners, to proclaim the year of the Lord's favor and the day of vengeance of our God, to comfort all who mourn, and provide for those who grieve in Zion — to bestow on them a crown of beauty instead of ashes, the oil of gladness instead of mourning, and a garment of praise instead of a spirit of despair. They will be called oaks of righteousness, a planting of the Lord for the display of his splendor. They will rebuild the ancient ruins and restore the places long devastated; they will renew the ruined cities that have been devastated for generations.

Isaiah 61:1-4

Instead of their shame, my people will receive a double portion, and instead of disgrace they will rejoice in their inheritance; and so they will inherit a double portion in their land, and everlasting joy will be theirs.

Isaiah 61:7

Jesus is saying to you today, "Come unto Me all you who labor and are heavy laden, pained and overburdened, and I will cause you to rest. I will ease and relieve and refresh your soul."

Run to Jesus. Give up the counterfeit comforters. Ask Him to show you where the pain is — the root issues in your life. Allow His Holy Spirit to invade your very being and begin to do surgery on you. God wants to rebuild your life. God wants to raise you up. The Great Physician is there with you now. He wants to renew you: spirit, soul and body. He wants to give you an overhaul. He wants to give you His peace that passes all understanding — joy unspeakable and full of glory.

Repent with these words, "Father, forgive me for not coming to You with my pain. Forgive me for trying to deal with the pain in my flesh. Redeem the time the enemy of my soul has stolen. Father, I thank You for making me a new person. I'm being made over again by Your Spirit."

One reminder to you: If you feel pain over something someone says, or something that someone does, and if you have a reaction, there is an area of your life that needs to be healed. You cannot continue to ignore that pain and blame others. You must look at yourself and have time for the pain. Deal with the pain and let the Lord come to the root in your life and take it out so you will be whole in that area. Search your heart today.

Chapter 4
Deadly Deception

Some Christian single women are content and happy being single. They don't feel a desperation to marry, but they are trusting God and just waiting on the promise. Others have decided they will probably never marry and don't feel compelled to do so. They are happy with their lives and marriage doesn't matter.

I find most often many single women are living in disappointment. As a woman who didn't marry until after I turned forty, I can relate to all three of those categories. I lived all three attitudes at different times in my life.

Honestly there are not many emotionally healthy single men available in the Christian community. But there are presently 88 million single people in America as recently reported by Dateline NBC.

I read an article once that said a single woman over forty is more likely to be struck by lightning than to get married. I was not discouraged by that article because I had a promise from God. The world's statistics are greater in the church because more women go to church than men. Just look around next Sunday and see for yourself, but don't be moved by that if you have a promise from God for marriage. I did not allow the world's statistics to move me when I began to seek God for a mate.

Disappointment is failure of an expectation, a miscarriage of a plan or design.[1] Disappointment comes when a plan to be married by a certain age does not happen. I wanted to marry in my twenties, but it did not happen.

Many young women begin to wonder what is wrong with them and why they are not married. They see others marrying and having children. They feel alone and left out. I got very frustrated. I was in so many weddings. I was the bridesmaid, the maid of honor, served punch and cake and received the guests. I planned the showers and helped my friends shop for their wedding trousseaus. It was painful.

Many of these disappointed women have been faithful to God and have made something of their lives, yet in the area of love they feel as though they have been thrown to the lions. The Bible says in Proverbs 13:12, "Hope deferred makes the heart sick, but a longing fulfilled is a tree of life."

Many young women today are heartsick because their hopes and dreams have not come into fruition. They have waited, and waited, and waited, and waited and yet nothing has happened.

I'll never forget one of my most painful moments when I was single. I went out to dinner with a married couple and their new baby girl. The husband had been a dear friend of mine and a co-laborer at Higher Dimensions Ministry. We had a great time.

They brought me back to my apartment and we were visiting about the ministry and about life. My

---

[1] Webster's II New Riverside University Dictionary, p. 382.

friend said, "Helen, you have such a fruitful life in the ministry, it's o.k. that you are single, because you are serving God and blessing a lot of people. Even if you never get married you're such a blessing. So don't worry about being single or getting married." We prayed together and they walked out of my door — him with his wife and new baby.

I shut the door behind them and there I was in my apartment, all alone and I cried out to God. I promised the Lord that when I married I would remain sensitive to the hurts and pains of singles. I'm not saying that my friend was insensitive, but when you are happily married it is easy to tell singles it's o.k. to be single. I was in my late thirties and they were still in their twenties — married with a baby. They couldn't relate to my pain.

This spirit of disappointment must be dealt with in our lives. We must go to God with our broken relationships or no relationships and ask God to fill us with Him. Cast all of our care upon Him for He cares for us. We must learn to love our lives and release our hopes and dreams to Him. We must learn to find joy in waiting for God's best.

We must be obedient to His voice and continue to be about our Father's business. "The vision is yet for an appointed time . . . though it tarry, wait for it" (Habakkuk 2:3 KJV).

I know a young woman who is presently living in disappointment. She believed she would have a mate by the end of last year. The year before that was supposed to be the year as well. Now she just stays at home and isn't even working. She doesn't attend church faithfully, yet she says she loves God.

She must believe that God is going to send her husband to her front door because even recently she said her husband was coming. Her disappointment has placed her in an unhealthy state. She has not been open to the Lord. If she were hearing His voice clearly over the voice of her biological clock and her own desire, she would hear His words of comfort. He would take her disappointment and give her strength to wait on His appointment.

Disappointment leads to despair. Despair is hopelessness and despondency. I have talked with so many single women who are at the point of despair. They know God can, but they really don't believe He will. They have gotten to the place where there is a feeling of futility. They have lost all confidence and faith in God. Some don't try to fix themselves up anymore — "What's the use?" is their attitude. They don't get involved in the work of the Lord or in their local church.

If this attitude of heart is not dealt with, it can lead women to suicide. It can also lead to a life filled with deception and delusion. These two spirits are taking many women by storm in the Body of Christ. They have allowed these spirits into their lives by not trusting God — they have become double-minded women, unstable in all of their ways (James 1:8). That which is not of faith is sin (Romans 14:23).

Many of these young women don't even realize they are in sin. They are not trusting God and have lost all faith and all hope. Everything they do is based on fear and doubt.

> **God hath not given us the spirit of fear; but of power, and of love, and of a sound mind.**
>
> **2 Timothy 1:7 KJV**

Traveling around the world with a single evangelist for many years opened my eyes to the spirit of deception that attacks women in the Christian community. At first when coming face to face with this issue, I just called it the crazy women's syndrome. "Oh no, not another one," I would say. Then time after time, woman after woman — the letters, the phone calls, the prophecies, would come into the ministry. I realized this was a spirit single women had allowed to attach itself to them.

Since our ministry team didn't stay in one place longer than a week, the spirit of deception would manifest itself through the mail and by the phone. Women wrote and called saying God had told them they were to be the evangelist's wife. They had received prophecies from reliable prophets and words from God from their pastors and friends. If we ministered in a certain area of the country for several weeks, these women would travel from church to church, sitting on the front row.

These women did not know the evangelist personally. Most of them had never had a conversation with him. They only knew the man they saw on the stage. I do believe that many times a woman sees a man moving in the anointing and she is drawn to the anointing she experiences during the meeting.

When the anointing is flowing, that is the ultimate spiritual experience. It is so precious, so fulfilling. One would love to experience that forever. It is at this point where I believe young Christian women get off course. They begin to see the individual as the object of that sweet spirit when it is really the anointing — the very Spirit of God.

You cannot be in love with someone with whom you have no personal relationship. You can be in lust or infatuated, but you cannot truly love someone you do not know. Love is a decision. You make a decision to love someone after getting to know them — their heart, mind and purpose.

People who fall in love with Jesus, fall in love with Him because they have a personal and intimate relationship with Him. Many churchgoers do not pray and are not seeking the deeper things of God. They are attending for a variety of reasons, but they are not in love with Jesus. They can't really love someone with whom they have no relationship.

When I was in my late twenties I had a dream that I was inside a convent filled with nuns and it was a very beautiful place, a place I felt comfortable, but God opened up a door and took me out of that place. I knew then that someday I would be married. Over the years I received various prophetic words that I would marry and I held on to some Scriptures. (The promise may come through the Word — or through a prophetic word.) However, God never told me who I was going to marry. He never told me his name, He just promised me a mate.

I have searched the Scriptures thoroughly and I find no place where God told a woman who her husband would be by name. There are many well-meaning friends and prophets who know your gifts and talents and they think you would make a great pastor or minister's wife. They see a single young man flowing in the gifts and they prophesied to you that this is the person for you. They are sincere — but often they are sincerely wrong. If they were correct, some of these single men of God would have had to marry over a thousand women because they have been promised to as many women in so-called prophecy.

When I began to really recognize this as a spirit on women in the church, I began to pray a covering over myself so that spirit would not attach itself to me. I asked God to cover my mind and emotions and not let me get off and fail in the task He had given me.

I was close to the single minister I worked with. He was my friend and brother and I knew God had called me to work with him and stand by his side. I did not want God's will to get mixed up with my flesh. God protected me. I never thought I was going to marry him, I knew God had someone for him and I knew God had someone for me.

I have seen critical cases of this disease over the years in ministry. I believe it is an epidemic and Satan has used this to hinder Christian women in their walk with God. I feel it is important to expose Satan and his lies.

The examples I will share with you will detail only a few of the misguided marriage-minded women I have seen over the years. These incidents did not all occur involving the ministry I was working in, but in several ministries with which we were associated. When ministers get together they share their horror stories and take some comfort in knowing that they are not alone in experiencing satanic attack.

I have changed the names and places to protect the identity of many of the young women who are still in need of deliverance.

Marci

A young single man started a church in the early 70's, and within the first few weeks a lovely young woman familiar with his ministry moved from North Dakota to be a part of his fellowship. She was articulate, well-groomed, attractive and loved to praise God. Marci sat on the front row every service and was demonstrative in her worship. She was sweet and was always available to help at every occasion.

Subtly she let her intentions be made known — she was "called" to be the pastor's wife. She befriended the staff and members of the pastor's family. She bought gifts and sent cards of encouragement. She invited staff members over to her home for gourmet meals. These things in themselves were good, however the motive was deceiving. Those who are deceived are deceptive.

The pastor was always as kind to her as he was to everyone. Some women misinterpreted his actions. They would say things like, "He told me he liked my dress. He said I looked pretty today. He shook my hand differently than he did everyone else. He starred at me during the whole service."

The last thing that was on the pastor's mind was one of these women. Nevertheless, you could not convince them otherwise. This particular young woman finally came to a place of desperation. She went to the pastor's home. He refused to come to the door since he was home alone. She went back and forth from her house to his all afternoon.

Finally, out of frustration the pastor asked one of his staff members to speak to her. She did not receive correction. She didn't want to hear the truth. She decided it was only the opinion of the messenger, not the minister, since he did not speak to her personally. Refusing to accept the truth, she tried to commit suicide. Right after she took the pills, she called the church hoping the pastor would come to her home and rescue her. Instead he sent several other staff ministers who took her to the hospital. The spirit of deception and delusion almost took her life. She finally moved to another city, away from the minister and to this day she has never married.

Katie

Katie had a great personality, but was not a very attractive woman. She had a good job, worked in the church and was loved by the people. She was involved in the singles group and met a young woman there whom she found out was good friends with a well-known single Christian entertainer. Katie befriended this woman and later when this woman moved away, Katie went to visit her. This just happened to be the same city where the single Gospel singer also lived.

After Katie visited, she told her friend she was moving there and had job interviews. People prayed for her to get the job. Upon returning home from her visit, she wore an engagement ring and new diamond earrings. She told her friends she was engaged to this man.

She had been introduced to him after one church service, but a hello and a handshake was all the "relationship" she had experienced. She had a complete breakdown when her move and planned marriage did not happen. She was institutionalized and several years later has still never married.

Linda

Linda was in her thirties. She had a stable job with the electric company where she had been employed for twenty years. She was divorced, but had no children. She became enamored with a television evangelist and began corresponding with him — at least she thought it was him. It was actually a staff minister in his office who handled his mail.

Most of the evangelists with large ministries read very little of their own mail, they do not have the time, but they have dedicated ministers who help them with their mail. This evangelist was having a week of meetings out of the country and invited his partners to come along. Linda saved her money and couldn't wait to have some personal interaction with this man — the man she believed was to be her mate.

At these meetings, Linda did get the opportunity to meet him personally and even take a photo with him. It was banquet night so all of the people were dressed up. Linda returned home from the meeting and had the snapshot enlarged. She told everyone this was their engagement picture. Linda also purchased a ring.

Linda planned a wedding, bought bridesmaids' dresses and went so far as to send one to the minister's sister. She called the evangelist's secretary and requested him to perform a wedding at a particular church on the date she had chosen for her marriage.

The evangelist was going to be out of the country on that date and the secretary informed the woman that he couldn't be there. This did not stop Linda — after all she had heard from God. On the planned wedding day, the cake arrived at the church along with the flowers and the bridal party. The maintenance man at the church explained to the bride's sister that no wedding had been scheduled for that day.

A pastor of the church dropped by who knew the evangelist and talked to them. He explained to the family that the evangelist barely knew the woman who was the so-called bride-to-be. Ninety guests arrived for the wedding with their printed invitations and gifts. The groom was noticeably absent. He heard from God too. He was in Europe, evangelizing where God had called him — not at the church marrying a woman he did not know.

This evangelist later started a church and was married but even after he was married, this woman was so deceived she still thought she was going to marry him. Linda still has her stable job and every other area of her life seems to be normal, but when it comes to this situation she is totally deceived. Today Linda still waits for this man to be her husband, believing she has heard from God.

Two Sisters

Two sisters who were dedicated prayer warriors believed two men who were in leadership at the church they attended were to be their husbands. One believed she was going to marry the children's pastor and the other one thought she was going to marry the youth pastor. They never got out of line, but they told their mother they were absolutely sure this was what God had told them.

Both of the men they were claiming married other women. Neither sister even dated one of these men.

It's been over ten years since the men married and still neither sister has married.

Polly

Polly, a never married single parent, had two daughters. She came into the church believing she was the one to marry the single pastor. She gave him gifts and was always sending flowers and cards. The pastoral staff wrote her a letter and asked her to stop. She said she wouldn't stop until she heard from the pastor for herself. Her daughters were telling people the pastor was their father. It was beginning to cause confusion in the church.

Finally, the pastor spoke directly with her. He informed her he was not interested in her as a mate. As she walked out the door, she turned and said, "I know you are liking me and you will marry me." A few years later she sat in the audience and watched as he married someone else. She has never married.

Kelli

Kelli was a married woman with several children. She was happily married, but had a dream that her husband died and she married a famous minister. She told her husband and he was caught up in the deception. He took her to this man's meetings and together they followed him to many cities. It looked so innocent, but she was controlled by a spirit of deception and delusion.

That minister is now happily married. Kelli's husband still lives and they are together today, however now she believes that his wife is also going to die and she will marry this man.

Lisa

Lisa is in her early forties. She has a college degree and has held many executive positions over the years. A dedicated Christian, she loves God with all of her heart. She comes from a good home, however in her single life, she too has fallen into the deception trap. She was prophesied to by someone years ago that she would marry a famous man in the Gospel and later someone actually prophesied a particular name to her.

Lisa believes this is going to happen. She has prayed for this man often. She has put out many fleeces, she has seen him on the freeway and in the local library. Prayer partners and pastors' wives have joined her in her deception. She believes that he stares at her and gives her special signs from the pulpit when she is in the audience.

She believes he thinks he isn't good enough for her and that makes him afraid to approach her. They have met on several occasions, but he never has asked for her phone number or pursued any sort of relationship with her. He recently married and is going on with his life. She has never married.

I could go on and on with these stories. They all have a similar strain. "He gives me special looks. He held my hand when he shook it. He stares at me. He calls me. He put me on his mailing list at my private mailbox number so obviously he has asked someone about me," not realizing that she signed a card at his service with her private address on it.

When it comes to women who are interested in ministers, most of these women think the minister personally answers their letters. When they receive an invitation to a conference, seminar or special meetings, they think he invited them personally. In reality, he personally invited everyone on his mailing list. Direct mail programs make letters look very personal. They are designed to make one feel they are reading a letter just for them when in fact the same letter may have been produced for forty-thousand partners of the ministry.

One woman said, "He gave me his personal 800 number and we have been talking daily." When she actually met the man in person he refused her gifts. She wept for hours, but still didn't get the message. They had never spoken. He told her, "I don't even know you, and what you are thinking is not right."

This spirit will consume your life. It inundates your thought life with lies. You will see him in a crowd and swear that he is looking at you. You will drive down the street and see him in his car and know it was God that you saw him at that moment.

I remember while attending Oral Roberts University how all the guys who were studying for the ministry wanted a girl who could play the piano and help them with their ministry. They would see a cute girl and would stand next to her in the cafeteria line. If he put mustard, mayo and pickles on his sandwich and she did the same, he'd say to himself, "I know it's God." If he was in her class and had the same type of notebook, he would say, "This has to be God. We are so much alike. She must be the one for me."

Don't allow disappointment and despair to lead you into deception. If you recognize yourself in any of the examples, ask God for deliverance. While you are claiming a certain man for your husband, you may be missing the very best one God has chosen for you. Maybe that man God has planned for you is right next door or at your job. Maybe he is very close, but you have your eyes on a particular someone else.

You don't know what is best for you. God knows what is best for you. Just because someone is good-looking and in the ministry doesn't mean that he is God's best for you.

Many women have believed that they were going to marry Pastor Carlton, but none of the ones who claimed him are married to him today. And it is also sad, none of the ones who claimed him have married yet, except those who have been delivered from the spirit of deception. "You will know the truth, and the truth will set you free" (John 8:32).

As long as you continue in this deception, God can't bring the right man into your life. If you talk to these young women, they will say, "I'm not off like all those others. This is a different situation. I've really heard from God about him." There is no way that God would promise all these women the same man. God is not the author of this kind of confusion (1 Corinthians 14:33).

"He who finds a wife finds what is good and receives favor from the Lord" (Proverbs 18:22). It is not a woman's place to find a husband. This is out of God's order.

There comes a time when single women must do a reality check. Women who are operating in a spirit of deception are not looking at themselves clearly. A handsome, important and famous man is not looking for a woman who doesn't fix herself up and doesn't have anything going for herself.

He is going to be attracted to women who are like him — attractive and outstanding. Most men initially choose or show interest in a woman according to what they first see. If what they see isn't attractive to them, they usually don't ask for a date.

I once asked Carman if there had ever been a woman he was interested in that he was afraid to call or approach. He said "No. Any woman I have been interested in, I approach them soon after I meet them. Helen, if I was interested in someone, believe me, I would do something about it." In other words, if you haven't been approached, he's not interested in you.

Single woman, there is no reason to be desperate. If God has someone for you, he will find you in God's timing and it will be wonderful. There is an old hymn that says, "You can't hurry God, oh no, you just have to wait. You have to trust Him and give Him time, no matter how long it takes. He's God and He doesn't hurry, He'll be there, don't you worry. He may not come when you want Him, but He's always right on time."

I know that for myself. I look back on relationships of my past and see my waiting allowed God to bring exactly the right one. The others were just preparation for what God had for me. Oh yes, I'm like every other woman, I would have liked to have been married at twenty, but that was not God's plan for my life. When I yielded to His, He brought His best for me.

God is faithful and He knows the desires of your heart. You must trust God and refuse to allow deception to rule your life. If you give in to deception, it brings delay. You could miss the will of God for your life because God cannot honor your deception.

If you are in this place, take your disappointments to God. Talk to Him about your pain. Cry out to Him. He will hear you and He will answer you (2 Chronicles 20:9). Repent for living in fear, doubt and unbelief. Ask God to give you the faith to wait for His will and His best for your life.

Deal with the root issues of your life. Begin to prepare yourself for God's best instead of fantasizing away your days. Allow the Holy Spirit to change you and make you whole. If necessary run, don't walk, to your nearest Christian counselor. Saturate your day in the Word of God. Play it in your sleep, read it when you are awake.

Replace your old conversation with the Word. Find out what God says about you and about your life. Line your life up with God's Word. Read Christian books and fill your mind with the good things. Read things that encourage you in your Christian walk and bring you closer to Him. Stay active in your church or ministry. Keep busy about the things of the Lord. Don't waste your time daydreaming about what could be.

If you keep busy and serve the Lord with all of your spirit, soul, mind and body — God will honor your faithfulness. "No good thing will he withhold from them that walk uprightly" (Psalm 84:11 KJV).

Stir up the gifts of God that are within you (2 Timothy 1:6). You were created by God and you have gifts no one else has. Stir up your gifts and use them for His glory. Your gifts will make room for you and bring you before great men (Proverbs 18:16). Stop concentrating on the *great men* and concentrate on THE GREAT MAN — the Giver of every good and perfect gift.

Pray, "God, I repent for being full of disappointment and despair. Forgive me for trying to do Your job in choosing my mate. You know what is best for me. Deliver me from any spirit of deception. I do not want to miss what You have planned for me."

Chapter 5
How To Find the Perfect Lover

May He grant you out of the rich treasury of His glory to be strengthened and reinforced with mighty power in the inner man by the [Holy] Spirit [Himself indwelling your innermost being and personality].

May Christ through your faith [actually] dwell (settle down, abide, make His permanent home) in your hearts! May you be rooted deep in love and founded securely on love.

That you may have the power and be strong to apprehend and grasp with all the saints [God's devoted people, the experience of that love] what is the breadth and length and height and depth [of it];

[That you may really come] to know [practically, through experience for yourselves] the love of Christ, which far surpasses mere knowledge [without experience]; that you may be filled [through all your being] unto all the fullness of God [may have the richest measure of the divine Presence, and become a body wholly filled and flooded with God Himself]!

Ephesians 3:16-19 AMP

Women, for the most part, are unequipped to handle a real love relationship. Many have never known wholeness in their life and home as a child. They have had no example of a real and lasting love relationship. Parents have divorced or there has been only one parent from the beginning. Friends and coworkers alike have not been examples of a healthy, loving relationship.

I can remember as a single woman looking around in a moment of honesty and evaluating the marriages of those nearest to me. At that time I found only two marriages I would have wanted to emulate. All the others, Christian and non-Christian alike, had some major issues that kept the couple from fulfillment.

My sister had one such marriage. She had married while still in college. Our father had died before either of us had become teenagers. Our maturing and dating years were spent with only the input of a mother who had stayed single until she was nearly forty since she had preferred serving God on the mission field to marriage. She had been married only thirteen years when our father died.

Looking for a strong man figure in her life, my sister chose the first man who could offer her security. She readily admits that she did not seek God on the matter. The choice looked like God. He was saved, raised in the same denomination (important prerequisite for a Christian girl), felt God had something for them to accomplish together (answering the cry of her spirit), and could offer her the security of a home and a family (answering the longing of her flesh).

JoAnne thought she was making a mature, godly choice in a mate, but she did not have all the facts and was too young to recognize some dysfunctional signs — in her husband's family as well as in her own psyche. She soon became a victim by her own choosing.

Love is a choice. You don't fall in love, you choose to love. When Jesus, our example of love, knocks on the door of our hearts, He never barges in. He is a gentleman. We have a choice to accept His love. We must choose to love and then develop a love relationship with Him just as we choose other relationships in our lives.

He first loved us. He knew the measure of our days before we were ever born (Psalm 139:15-18). He called us and chose us (Hosea 2:14-16,19,20). He knows us so well He has even numbered the hairs on our head (Matthew 10:30). He died that we might have life (John 3:16). He rejoices over us (Isaiah 62:5). His love is everlasting (Jeremiah 31:3). And He longs to be your lover and your husband (Isaiah 62:1,3,4). We are His "Hephzibah." His delight is in us (vv. 5,6).

Jesus is the original "romantic." He was wooing us before we came to be. The Song of Solomon presents a typology of that kind of love for us in the story of the Shunammite woman and her shepherd. *Shunammite* means "the following." How much more do we need to know to recognize ourselves in this passage?

Our first love is not only a romantic, but He has given us some incredible tools with which to chose and develop our love.

One of the most misused tools is the ability to fantasize. Fantasy is nothing more than creative imagination. It is an attribute of God. How else could He have dreamed up this world and its inhabitants? He was a dreamer and a planner. Fantasize in its root comes from the Greek and means "to make visible." When you begin to visualize something in your mind you start to plan your life around it. Fantastic ideas come from fantasy.

Unfortunately, this God-given gift of fantasy has been so misused that it is almost considered a dirty word in the Kingdom of God. We have shied away from teaching the creative, positive ways to use this gift. The Word tells us in the most simple terms, "As he thinketh in his heart, so is he" (Proverbs 23:7 KJV).

Many women have spiritualized their fantasy of one certain man for their lives. They spend hours visualizing situations with that man. They write poetry and letters. They try to find out his favorite color. They are continually planning a way to run into him at his next meeting or concert. Since the faith message has been so widely taught, now they drive by his house, claiming him for their own.

Women spend hours conniving to get his phone number and show up at his office. They send gifts and flowers to a man they have never met or perhaps have met once in passing. They dream of his response when he receives them.

From personal experience I can tell you that most famous men (both in the secular and in the spiritual communities) never see the gifts that are sent. Generally the staff person assigned to the mail handles all the personal responses, and the man who already has everything donates all gifts.

It may seem inconsiderate to some however, especially in the case of ministry, a man of God cannot be consumed with fan mail. He has to concentrate on the things of God and be in fasting and prayer. His concern is the ministry.

Most of the ties and cuff links Pastor Carlton received as gifts went to members of staff or family. He would not wear them in ministry because it could give false hope to some young woman who was believing God for him to become her husband.

Jesus is jealous over you (2 Corinthians 11:2). He does not want you to exult someone over Him. When you spend hours dreaming of anyone or anything, it becomes an idol in your life and you are violating the first of all the commandants. How have we deceived ourselves into thinking that God will give us that idol?

My sister recently attended a concert where a 1970's Motown group was performing. The men were still sharp in their matching suits. They were delightful and entertaining. The one original member still had all his vocal range and didn't miss a step in the choreographed moves.

At one point during the concert they brought a number of women on stage. They started singing to the women and one in particular began to weep as the lead singer sang directly to her. She held her hand over her mouth to muffle the sobs and raised her hand as if she were in praise and worship to this most high and unholy singer. How tragic that this idol received praise and glory that is to be reserved only for God.

It is time for women of God to refocus. You may have been feeling pretty holy. You don't dance, you don't drink and you don't dress like a common hooker. You go to church every time the doors are open, and except for one or two little indiscretions (that have been forgiven), you have lived a holy life.

The church at Ephesus had done all the right things. They had worked hard and persevered. They did not tolerate wickedness. They had not become weary in well-doing, but they had lost their first love (Revelation 2:2-4). They had been making idols of silver and worshipping them. The goddess Diana, whose name means "complete light," had become a focus of their worship and a livelihood for many (Acts 19). The church was focusing on the wrong light. They had forgotten The Light of the World, Jesus.

The entire Body of Christ needs to hear this message, but for single women today it is a poignant word. We must get our eyes off anything that takes the place of our first love.

Several years into her marriage, my sister realized there was a great emptiness inside. Her emotional needs were not being met. Her husband only reacted the way he knew from the dysfunction of his upbringing. Being the good Christian girl that she was and recognizing that divorce was not an option, she chose to stick with it.

To keep her sanity and salvation something had to change, and that change occurred on the inside — in her spirit. She had been clinging to the Word of God, filling her home with praise and worship and listening to ministry tapes to keep her sanity. "I may not have the love of my life that I longed for, but I do have the Lover of my soul," she declared.

On a trip to Denver, Colorado, she made a purchase to seal her commitment to the Lover of her soul. She bought a ring with a heart and the word Jesus on it in gold. It meant more to her than the beautiful attention-getting wedding ring she wore. She never took off her ring of commitment to the Lover of her soul.

When she needed attention, she would take a mental walk on the beach, hand in hand with the Lover of her soul. She would share every little detail of her day with Him. She asked His opinion on everything and though she sometimes reacted to circumstances in her flesh, her Lover never left her.

JoAnne came to know the unconditional love of God for the first time. She never got too fat for His love. He didn't stop caring if she said too much in anger. When she misunderstood or mismanaged He was still there. He would walk with her and talk with her any hour of the day or night. She only had to reach out for Him and He was there.

She wrote to Him in her journal — words of love, feelings of hurt — whatever was on her heart and He was never critical. She practiced and developed the ultimate love relationship.

When we have a man in our lives, we often spend every waking minute thinking of how to please him. We buy clothes, fix our hair and makeup the way he likes it. We wear his favorite fragrance and can hardly pass a rack of cards without looking for something that expresses to him how we feel. A woman will slave over a hot stove and spend hours sweating in the gym for the man in her life. He becomes the focus for existence.

We dream of our wedding day, name the children to come and design the perfect house. We think of every possible perfect honeymoon place and see ourselves walking along the beach, climbing mountains, strolling under the Eiffel Tower, and riding in a gondola in Venice.

The same imagination we use to dream of this love we can use to focus on the Lover of our soul. We need to make Jesus more real in our lives. We must listen for His voice and long to hear each word that comes from Him. His love letter to us is the Word. We should hold it close to our heart, read it over and over and sleep with it. The words of your Lover should be the first thing you long to hear in the morning and the last thing you long to hear at night.

Cultivate your love relationship with the Lover of your soul. Visualize Him beside you in the car, at work and when you are shopping. The Lover of my soul even knows where all the bargains are and will direct me there if I simply let Him.

My sister was married for eighteen years and the Lord sustained her until the day her husband chose divorce. Jesus continued to be the Lover of her soul. She did not have to grab on to Him at the last minute, because she had already made Him the Lover of her soul.

As a single parent she often needed the guidance of her Lover. He now also became provider as her earthly security had been removed. In November one year she had to go shopping for a friend. She did some of his Christmas shopping as he had a huge list and was busy with his ministry.

While looking for dresses for his sisters, JoAnne found a dress that was perfectly her. It called her name (you know what I mean, ladies!). She was struggling financially and there was no money for a dress. Making the purchases for her friend, she left the store, but not without first talking back to that dress. "I know you are meant to be mine, see you later."

In February of the following year she had received a little blessing financially and she decided to go back to that store and buy that dress. Well, of course, the entire store had been changed around. The dress was no longer where it once was. Under her breath she fumed, "Someone in Tulsa is walking around wearing my dress."

Though disappointed she wandered through the store speaking to the Lover of her soul. "I know that no dress can be important enough to separate me from You, Lord. I love You with or without that dress. No dress will dictate how I feel or control my attitude. I know You have only the best in mind for me."

As she neared the door she passed a rack of markdowns. The sign on the end of the rack said, "An additional 33 percent off at the register." Laughing at the "junk" on that rack, my sister began to move the garments hanger by hanger. "Torn. Makeup stained. Who would be caught dead in that?" she said as she filed through. Then one hanger away from leaving the store she gasped. "My dress," she cried.

There was nothing wrong with it — no tears, no stains, nothing. It was perfect and it was only $23 now when originally it had been well over $100.

How she laughed and rejoiced with the Lover of her soul as she walked out of the store with that dress. Whenever she wore it and got compliments — it was her — she told her friends her Lover had given it to her.

JoAnne did not always have happy days. There were many difficult, dark times to endure, but she never lost the relationship with that Lover. Even at times when her sons were away with their father and she was alone, she would joke that she lived with three guys — The Father, the Son and the Holy Ghost.

Her love relationship with Jesus continues today. After twelve years of singleness, God gave her a new husband. He is not jealous of her Lover. He knows that her love relationship with Jesus makes her more equipped to live whole in the marriage God has given them.

Once you have had the ultimate love relationship — that is with the Lover of your soul — then you will be better able to recognize the love of your life when the Lord sends him your way. Remember the Word, "Seek ye first the kingdom of God, and his righteousness; and all these things shall be added unto you"? (Matthew 6:33).

As you allow Jesus to be the Lover of your soul, things will begin to change in your life. Your life will be wrapped up in pleasing Him and not in pleasing a man. You'll find your very nature changing. Not only must He be the Lover of your soul, but He must become the Lover over your entire being.

When I was a young girl, I remember asking my mother why women wore white dresses as the bride. My mother responded by saying that they had kept themselves pure. I didn't know what it meant at the time, but I made a decision that I was going to deserve the white dress I would wear down the aisle someday.

Growing up and beginning to date, I realized that it was a choice for me to have or not to have premarital sex with someone. People who say, "It just happened, and before we knew it we were "doing it,'" are lying. It takes time to take off your clothes, and having premarital sex is a choice. They had time to think about their decision. Christians who respond by saying, "It's just a natural thing," are choosing not to follow the Scriptures. "Be ye holy; for I am holy"

(1 Peter 1:16 KJV). "Flee from sexual immorality" (1 Corinthians 6:18). "Abstain from all appearance of evil" (1 Thessalonians 5:22 KJV). Yes, it is natural, but it is to be in the confines of marriage. "Marriage is honourable in all, and the bed undefiled" (Hebrews 13:4 KJV).

I chose to make Jesus the Lover of my soul and save myself for the man that God brought into my life. I'm not going to say that it was always an easy choice, because we are human beings with emotions. However, using our humanness to justify our sin doesn't work with God. I'm happy for women who testify that they lived a life of immorality and now they are right. Praise God for that, but we need more women who will stand up and say, "I lived pure until I married and when I walked down the aisle, I walked down to meet my husband as a virgin. He is blessed in that he will never have to share my memories of sexual encounters with other men from my past because I don't have any. He will never be threatened by any sexually transmitted disease, because the only man I have been with and will be with until death do us part is him."

I don't know where you have come from and I do not know your circumstances or your past. I don't know how many boyfriends you have had or perhaps how many sexual partners you have had. God is a forgiving God and He forgives you of past mistakes. But this I do know, from this day forward you can make a decision and make a commitment to the Lord that you will abstain from all sexual immorality and premarital sex and will not participate in those behaviors and activities. And when God brings you your husband, you can walk down that aisle in a white dress completely restored by the Holy Spirit as if you had never been with anyone before. You can present yourself to him as a bride without spot or wrinkle, washed in the blood of the Lamb.

And even when the Lord blesses you with a husband, the Lord will always be the Lover of your soul if you allow Him to be. I love my husband, I thank God for him every day. It is a joy to be married to such a wonderful man. But if they called me tomorrow and told me that he was dead, I would weep and I would cry and I imagine that I would have a few questions for the Lord. But I would go on and live my life for Jesus, the Lover of my soul. No one understands you and will ever love you as Jesus loves you. No matter how great the relationship, God made you and He knows all about you and He loves you in spite of you. Allow Him to become the Lover of your soul and the Lover of your entire life.

Several years ago I found a reading that I have often used in ministry. I do not know who wrote it originally, but obviously it was someone who clearly heard from God. I share it with you now. I pray it will impact your life. I pray idols will come down and Jesus will be lifted up in your life as you are challenged by this word.

On His Plan for Your Mate

Everyone longs to give themselves completely to someone — to have a deep soul relationship with another, to be loved thoroughly and exclusively.

But God, to a Christian says, "No, not until you are satisfied, fulfilled and content with being loved by Me. With giving yourself totally and unreservedly to Me, to having an intensely personal and unique relationship with Me alone. You will discover that only in Me is your satisfaction to be found, then you will be capable of the perfect human relationship that I have planned for you.

"You will never be rightfully united with another until you are united with Me, exclusive of anyone or anything else, exclusive of any other desires or longing. I want you to stop planning, stop wishing, and allow Me to give you the most thrilling plan existing — one that you cannot imagine.

"I want to give you the best. Please allow Me to bring it to you, just keep watching Me, expecting the greatest things, keep experiencing the satisfaction that I AM. Keep listening and learning the things I tell you.

"You just wait. That is all. Don't be anxious. Do not worry. Do not look around at the things others have gotten or that I have given them. Do not look at the things you think you want.

You just keep looking off and away up to Me or you will miss what I want to show you.

"And when you are ready, I will surprise you with a love far more wonderful than any you would ever dream. You see, until you are ready, (I am working even this moment to have you both ready together), until you are both satisfied exclusively with Me and the life I have prepared for you, you won't be able to experience the love that exemplified your relationship with Me. It is the only perfect love.

"I want you to see in the flesh, a picture of your relationship with Me, and enjoy materially and concretely the everlasting union of beauty, perfection and love that I offer you. Believe it and be satisfied."

Chapter 6
Can You Wait Just One More Hour?

It may be helpful to remind ourselves of the restoration found in pain. The pain you're presently feeling will work for good in your life if you will hold on and trust God.

The passage you are about to read comes from the most painful hour of Jesus' life — the hours just before He was captured by soldiers, taken to Pilate and ultimately to His death on the cross. This is the place where He said yes to God, and yes to the birthing pains for the redemption of mankind.

> Then Jesus went with his disciples to a place called Gethsemane, and he said to them, "Sit here while I go over there and pray." He took Peter and the two sons of Zebedee along with him, and he began to be sorrowful and troubled. Then He said to them, "My soul is overwhelmed with sorrow to the point of death. Stay here and keep watch with me."
>
> Going a little farther, he fell with his face to the ground and prayed, "My father, if it is possible, may this cup be taken from me. Yet not as I will, but as you will."
>
> Then he returned to his disciples and found them sleeping. "Could you men not watch with me for one hour?" he asked Peter. "Watch and pray so that you will not fall into temptation. The spirit indeed is willing, but the body is weak."
>
> Matthew 26:36-41

This scripture was given to me through my friend Sue at the most difficult time in my life. Pastor Carlton had just gotten married and I was thrilled for him, but I had always hoped I would be the first of the two of us to marry. My mother died two weeks later and I felt like an orphan. I felt like giving up. I was wondering if God's promises were going to come to pass in my life.

Even though I was walking in faith, there were times of loneliness, pain and wondering that I had to go through. One evening in late October, my phone rang. It was Sue and she said, "Helen, the Lord told me to ask you, 'Can you wait just one more hour?' Helen, He is about to do for you what He has promised. But you have to wait just a little while longer." She then read me the passage you have just read.

Jesus went with His disciples to a place called Gethsemane. *Gethsemane* means "olive press." A lot of us today are in the press. Everything is being crushed that can be crushed. We've had losses, hurts and disappointments. We are in Gethsemane. But the pressure of the press is allowing the anointing oil to flow from our lives. The more we allow God to press us in this hour and the more we line up with His Word and allow His character and nature to grow in us, the more the oil of the anointing will flow from our lives.

That anointing oil will flow in you, through you and over you. Things that once hurt you will slide right off. When relationships break up, your church splits, or you lose your job, the anointing will cause you to go through the crisis without feeling devastated. Literally those things will slide off. You become greasy with the anointing. Words — gossip, slander, people's opinions — slide off of you. Nothing negative can stick.

Jesus had that type of anointing on Him. When they tried to throw Him off the brow of the hill, the Bible tells us He walked through the crowd. He just slipped away and they did not know how. He walked in the anointing (Luke 4:29,30).

I have never had a baby, but I have coached women in the labor and delivery room. The last hour just before the baby is born is the most painful. The woman has endured nine months of changes in her body. She may feel fat and unattractive. Her hormones are raging and she has been on an emotional roller coaster. Even in the delivery room, she gets mad at her husband who is trying to assist her with the birth.

Now just before the baby is born, there is a painful process to endure. It is the most painful of the nine months' process, breathing, pushing, waiting and focusing. When the baby begins its journey through the birth canal its little body is being pushed out. The mother's pain is excruciating — but a baby is about to be born.

Jesus went through tremendous pain because He was giving birth to our redemption. This baby was not about to be born in an easy manner or fashion. In this last hour while they were in the olive press, Jesus looked at the disciples and told them to sit. I believe the reason He told them to sit was because He understood the pain and emotional drain of this last hour. I know the Scripture says when you've done all to stand, stand (Ephesians 6:13), but have you ever heard of anyone having a baby standing up?

Jesus knew the birthing process was painful. He knows that it will be painful for you as well. So go, sit down, rest on the Rock, Christ Jesus. Sit, and while you're sitting, allow your spirit to stand on His promises.

Jesus said, "Sit here, while I go over there and pray" (Matthew 26:36). Jesus knows that there are times in your life when the pain is so bad that you can barely utter a word in prayer. Sometimes I have been in a place where all I could say was, "Oh, oh, oh." The Bible says that when we moan and grown in the Spirit, He understands and that we are praying according to the will of God. Even when we don't know what to pray for and we can't form the words, the Spirit makes intercession with moaning and with groaning (Romans 8:26,27 KJV).

One of my favorite stories that Pastor Carlton tells is one about when he was still a teenager, evangelizing in California. He was having a revival several hours away from his home in San Diego. Every day during the week he'd go to school and in the afternoon he would come home and pray for an hour and then get dressed and drive to Barstow for revival.

One afternoon he came in and he was exhausted from fasting, praying and traveling every night. He started to get down on his knees to pray for the meetings and the Holy Ghost said, "Carlton, you take a nap, I'll pray for you."

He laid his head on the pillow and fell asleep. While he was sleeping, he was awakened by somebody praying. He heard someone singing in the Spirit and praying for the meeting. It was so sweet, he could feel the presence of the Lord. He thought his sister Tanya has come into the room and was praying at the foot of his bed.

He opened up his eyes. It wasn't Tanya, but a

figure he didn't recognize. It was someone in a long white robe. God had sent angels to pray. The Bible says in Isaiah 62 that the Lord has set watchmen on our walls and they will never give up or be silent day or night till our righteousness shines out like the dawn and our salvation like a blazing torch.

You have watchmen on the walls of your life. They may not know you, they may not know your name, but they are praying for you. And they are not going to stop praying. They've been given an assignment from heaven and they are not going to stop until God's purposes are fulfilled in your life.

God will send the hosts of heaven to protect and direct you. We have a High Priest who sits at the right hand of the Father and it is His job to ever intercede for us. That is what He is doing right now (Hebrews 7:25 KJV).

Jesus began to be sorrowful and troubled even to the point of death. He was about to give birth, so He was at the point of death. They say the closest a woman comes to death in the natural is when she is giving birth. If you are feeling that intense pain, you are about to give birth to something.

Jesus looked at the disciples once more and told them to stay put. He told them to stay "here" because it is the tendency of man to run from pain. When things get tough in a relationship, we run. Painful situations take place in the church and we leave. When things become uncomfortable on our job, we quit. We spend our lives running from the pain. We really just need to run to Jesus, the great pain reliever. If you keep running from the pain, you will never be set free.

I remember coaching a young single woman who was having a baby. She was in tremendous pain and she kept saying, "I don't want this. Stop this. I don't want this." The birthing process was so difficult. I said back to her, "Honey, that's what you should have told that man nine months ago . . . 'I don't want this,' — then you wouldn't be having this pain right now."

You asked God for a new job, a new car or a husband. You've asked Him for some things and He's made you some promises, but with every promise there is a condition. Once the conditions are filled by you, then God goes to work.

When the birthing process comes, it's painful. But don't abort the process by being unwilling to go through it. To get the promise you must go through the process. Stay put through the pain and allow God to do His work.

He told His disciples to keep watch. The reason He had to remind them to keep watch was because He knew their tendency to watch the circumstances. Get your eyes off the circumstances and off the situation and get your eyes on Jesus.

I pray for God to give me spiritual contact lenses. "God, somehow let me see what You are seeing in this situation." You must stay focused on Him. Many times in the delivery room the nurse will tell the woman to keep her eyes on a picture or on the exit sign — something to help her stay focused.

You need to keep focused on Jesus and on what His Word says. Keep watch with the Lord. Many women's hearts are failing them right now because of fear. They have their eyes on their age, on their looks, or on another's happy life. Their focus has been in the wrong place.

The Word says that God will keep you in perfect peace when your mind is stayed on Him (Isaiah 26:3 KJV). This passage gives us direct lessons regarding the do's and don'ts just before the promise comes forth — just before the baby is to be born.

Then Peter got into the flesh. He couldn't deal with the pain and the thought of losing Jesus, so he took out a sword and cut off a man's ear. If we get in the flesh, we sometimes abort the very promise God has for us.

Many single women with a promise from God for a husband simply get tired of waiting. They wait and wait and begin to feel like the old maid of the century, so they take matters into their own hands. They go out and find someone who is not saved and mess up the perfect will of God for their lives. They miss the mate God has been preparing for them.

Every decision you make in the flesh will affect the rest of your life. Seeds sown in the flesh reap a fleshly harvest. Today the earth continues to reap a harvest of evil because one woman got into her flesh — Sarah got tired of waiting. After all, she had waited twelve years and the promise was not yet fulfilled. So she did something on her own. But twenty-five years after the promise was given, God came through and did what He had said. Today the seed of Sarah's flesh and the promised seed are still fighting in the Middle East — Two half-brothers fighting over daddy's land. All because one woman got in the flesh when she failed to hold on to the promised word from God.

Watch your flesh while you are waiting — keep it in check. Beef up your spirit with the things of God. Learn to walk by faith and not by sight. Learn how to breathe through this time, learn how to wait, learn when it's time to push and always stay focused.

I remember an incident that occurred just a few short months before I became engaged. I had gone to California to the Azusa Conference we were having there. I had made plans to visit with Tim (a long time, good friend) after the conference. After I arrived in California I found that I could not exchange my ticket without paying an additional $400. Because of that, I now had only one day to spend with Tim.

We had been getting closer and I felt in my spirit that it was just a matter of time when we would be married, but I never breathed one word to anybody, not even to my closest friends.

We spent the day together and went for breakfast at the beach. I was stressed and wanted to be by the water to calm my spirit. I was mad because we only had one day together. Also, I was mad at God and Tim for not making a move toward a permanent commitment.

After breakfast we took a walk along the shore. We were looking at all of the names on the yachts. We were making fun of some of the names like "Miss Nellie Belle" and "Miss Lucy Pooh." We were on our way back to the car when I felt the Lord tell me to turn around. When I turned and looked, on the back of one of those yachts were the words "Trust Me." In my spirit I responded with "O.K., Lord, I will trust You. I will not get in the flesh. I will stay in the Spirit."

God is reminding you just now, if you have a promise from Him for marriage, you can trust Him. No matter how old you are, continue to have faith in His Word. With God nothing is impossible. It may seem like an impossible situation, but it is not difficult for God. Nothing is too hard for Him (Jeremiah 32:17).

Often we tell God how much we love Him, but do you trust Him as much as you love Him? Sing to yourself from the precious old hymn, "'Tis so sweet to trust in Jesus, just to take Him at His word."

In the last hour, you must not do what Judas did. Judas betrayed Jesus. In my opinion Judas betrayed Jesus because he didn't understand who Jesus really was. He thought that Jesus was going to set up an earthly kingdom, not a heavenly one. Therefore, you must not misunderstand the Lord during this season in your life. You must not become critical and bitter at God because He hasn't done things the way you thought He should.

You may have experienced some real disappointments and you are still blaming God. Let God have His will and His way in your life. Quit telling God how and when He should do what you want Him to do. I am reminded of the words to an old chorus we used to sing in church, "Let the Lord have His way in your life everyday, there's no rest, there's no peace until the Lord has His way. Place your life in His hands, rest secure in His plans. Let the Lord, let the Lord have His way."

Peter denied Jesus in those last moments. It is very easy when you're hurting to deny the word God gave you. It is easy to say, "It is not true, it's not going to happen." When the woman whom Elisha was staying with heard his prophecy that she was going to have a baby, she said back to him, "My lord, don't give me false hopes" (2 Kings 4:16).

I had received prophecies about marriage for years. There were times when I said, "I don't want to hear any more messages, I want the manifestation." Don't allow yourself to deny what God has promised. The devil doesn't care if you keep coming to church, sing in the choir and go to every prayer meeting. If he can get you to deny what God has said to you, then he has got you right where he wants you — in fear, doubt and unbelief.

When John baptized Jesus, the Spirit of the Lord came down from heaven and said, "This is my beloved Son, in whom I am well pleased" (Matthew 3:17 KJV). One verse later, the Spirit of the Lord drove Jesus into the wilderness. See, you can't have a message without first having a mess. You can't have a testimony without first having a test.

When the Word of God comes to you, the first thing that comes is the devil. He comes to steal, kill and destroy your faith, hope and promise. Just when you have received a prophecy that you are going to marry, you and your boyfriend break up. Receive a prophecy that you are getting a promotion and you lose your job. The devil will come to test the Word.

The devil said to Jesus, "If you are the Son of God, tell these stones to become bread" (Matthew 4:3). Satan knew Jesus could do miracles. He wanted to get Jesus to deny that He was the Son of God. He wanted to raise the question — if You really are the Son of God, why would He leave you out here in this wilderness?

And Satan's tricks continue today — if God really told you that you were going to marry, don't you think He would have given you a husband by the time you were twenty-five? Where is God? Why hasn't He done what He promised you? God doesn't care about you.

I remember the devil trying to lie to me many times. One day I was driving in a limousine down the street, going to pick up one of our church guests. We had a member of the church who owned several limousines. I was going to be our guest's host for the weekend, so we were picking her up in style. I was sitting in the front seat of the limo and up pulled a guy I used to date. He recognized me and waved.

The devil started talking, "See, that's another one you missed. God doesn't care about you. You are thirty something years old, and God is not going to come through for you."

But almost in an instant the Lord spoke to me. This guy was driving a Thunderbird. The Lord said to me, "You wanted a Thunderbird, but I'm going to give you a limousine." I said, "Thank-You, Lord." The Lord did give me a limousine.

Interestingly enough, just a few months before I was engaged, I was driving towards the Chicago Airport and I counted over twenty-seven limousines. The Lord said, "Helen, let this be a sign, your limo is on the way."

Remember this and don't you forget it!! The devil is a liar. He wants to get you to deny God's word through the prophet. He will tell you that you are never going to be happy and that you will never be fulfilled. Don't believe the devil's lie. God is about to birth something in you. God is about to bring forth a promise. Believe in the Son of God. Believe what He said to you.

God is not a man, that he should lie; neither the son of man, that he should repent: hath he said, and shall he not do it?

Numbers 23:19 KJV

My pastor married in September of 1993. I was happy for him. I hosted two bridal showers for Gina and spoke at their wedding. It was a joy to be a part of God's blessing in his life. This left me as the only single member of the pastoral staff. At every pastors' meeting I had to listen to everyone talking about their husbands and wives. I'm not going to lie, it hurt. I smiled, but I went home some nights and cried out to God.

At Pastor Carlton's wedding reception, Lindsay Roberts came to me. She said, "Helen, the Lord sent me here to the reception. I went home because I wasn't feeling well, but the Lord told me to come here and tell you something. The Lord told me to tell you to get ready, you're going to get married. He has seen your faithfulness and He is about to bless you. The Lord told me to tell you to go buy earrings for your honeymoon, do something in faith."

Now, I'm not a hyper-spiritual person and because of all I have seen over the years in ministry, I certainly do not believe in naming and claiming any particular man. I don't believe in buying a wedding dress and all this kind of stuff simply based on my hope that one day I will get married. But this was a direct word from God. She said, "Go do it. The Lord says go do it. Do something in faith."

Two days later Myles Monroe prophesied to me

and said, "Helen, the blessing that the pastor just got, you're getting ready to get it too. Your groom is coming."

Just two weeks later my mother passed away. She had been ill with Alzheimer's disease and had been in a nursing facility for several years. But with her death, I felt like an orphan. I didn't feel like I had anybody. I felt I had lost my covering.

Because of the depth of my mother's spiritual life, I now believe that she knew in her spirit. She had prayed for both Pastor Carlton and me to marry and he had just married, and my engagement was soon to come.

On my mother's funeral program, it stated that she died on November 16th instead of September 16th. My friend Sue came to me and said the error was not an accident. "The Lord told me to tell you on November 16th or directly after, there's going to be a marvelous breakthrough in your life and I think it's your husband."

There were times that my faith wavered, but I would pick myself back up and say, "God, I trust You through the pain and through the loneliness." Several times I found myself wishing that I wouldn't live another year like that particular year. I wasn't suicidal, but I want you to know the reality of what the enemy tries to put on us once we have received a word from God. The devil comes to *de* you — defeat, depress, destroy, demean, deceive, and delude. Jesus comes to *re* you — restore, redeem, revive, replenish, renew and refresh you.

November first came and Pastor Carlton called to ask me to go to California for a missions convention. At the time I had been away for my mother's funeral and a couple of speaking engagements. I had been out of the country for a Carman video shoot and I just didn't feel it was time for another trip. But he was insistent. The convention was being held in Pasadena, California, just twenty minutes away from Tim's house.

I tried to call Tim and let him know that I would be coming out to California, and was hoping we could get together. He had visited me in Tulsa several times and I would go to California and visit him. We were very close friends and had spent a lot of time together, but not in a dating relationship. Other than a slight peck on the lips, Tim had never really kissed me.

Tim wasn't home for the entire week before the conference, so I assumed I was in the flesh by trying to call him and maybe it wasn't God's will for us to see each other while I was there.

Before I phoned one last time, I prayed and asked God not to let Tim be at home if we were not supposed to get together. If he didn't answer this time I told the Lord I would accept His will in this circumstance and I wouldn't even call Tim when I arrived in California. I dialed once more and he answered on the first ring.

He said, "It's good to hear your voice, I've been on vacation." I told him that I was coming to Pasadena, and he asked me if we could go out to dinner on Monday night. I said yes.

The night before I left, my friend Dorothy called and out of the blue she said, "I think you are going to meet your husband this week." I said, "Sure, Dorothy, maybe I will."

The conference started November 14th. When I arrived at the hotel in Pasadena, Tim was there to meet me. We went out for dinner Monday and Tuesday nights, and on Wednesday night we went to hear Pastor Carlton preach at a church in Los Angeles. Pastor had just gotten married so he was sharing his testimony with the audience.

That night two people asked me if Tim was my boyfriend and if we were engaged. Godmother Campbell (Carlton's godmother) said, "That man is in love with you, Helen." I passed off her remark with a laugh.

A friend of ours in the ministry needed counseling and Pastor Carlton asked me to stay over in California to minister to the wife of the Pastor. Tim wanted to take me to dinner again, but I couldn't go due to the counseling situation. I told him that I could have breakfast with him before catching a plane the next morning.

Ready for a two-hour flight, dressed in a baseball cap and jeans, I met Tim for breakfast, except we never did eat anything. He started the conversation with, "Helen, I'm getting tired of this." "Tired of what?" I asked. He answered, "I'm getting tired of coming to Tulsa and leaving you, and I'm getting tired of you coming to California and leaving me."

My response was, "Oh, Tim, we'll always be close, we'll always be good friends." I responded that way for two reasons. First, to protect myself as I wasn't sure what he was going to say next. Secondly, because of a past relationship where I had never really known where I stood with the guy. I wanted Tim to make it plain as to exactly what he meant.

He said, "Well, I don't want to be friends. I love you and I want to marry you. I'm putting my house up for sale and I'm going to move to Tulsa. Whatever it takes. If it takes us six months, if it takes us a year, we'll go to counseling, we'll do whatever, but I'm not going to live without you anymore."

Then he said, "Helen, when we were in church Wednesday night and Pastor Carlton was telling his story about being engaged, he said that his godmother told him, 'Don't let her leave town without a ring,' I knew God was speaking to me and I'm not going to let you leave town without a ring." Out of his pocket came a beautiful box containing a gorgeous engagement ring.

Tim and I had known each other for twelve years. He had been a part of Higher Dimensions Church in its early stages. Pastor Carlton knew him well. We had all done things together during the years Tim had lived in Tulsa. Tim had seen me fat and skinny, up and down, happy and depressed. He saw me when I was lonely and hurting. He counseled me on other relationships and talked to me about my boyfriends ("jerks," he called them). He was right.

Tim knew I had a call on my life to preach and to minister. He was always sensitive to my needs over the years and it seemed that every time I was going through something, he would sense it and call me. Our friend-ship was a wonderful foundation for our courtship which was really our engagement time.

God was so faithful to give me a man with the char-acter of God just like I'd prayed. I knew he would stay my friend after so many years and that he knew the good and bad in me, yet loved me still.

If God can do it for me, He can do it for you. Trust Him. God is no respecter of persons. He loves you and wants to give you His best. Remember, "No good thing will he withhold from them that walk uprightly" (Psalm 84:11).

Let's pray. Father, we repent today for doubt and unbelief. We repent for not believing You will come through with what You have promised. Forgive us. Forgive us for not believing You and not believing in the gift of God within us. I pray for the women who are reading this book, show them who they are in You, God. Help them to walk in their calling and purpose. I pray they will know who they are, see how beautiful they are and how special they are to You.

I trust You, Lord, and I thank You. Lord, we lean and depend on You. We make a decision today to trust You. We make a decision to wait on You. While we're waiting on You we are going to submit our will to Your will and our purposes to Your divine purpose. We will mount up with wings as eagles. We will run and not be weary and we will walk and not faint. We will soar higher and higher in You. Today we say YES — Yes to Your will, yes to Your voice.

You're a God who is true to His Word and to His promise. You will do what You have said You will do. Father, I pray for my sisters. Lift them in the spirit of their mind and encourage their hearts this day. I speak hope into their lives. May they keep hope alive and keep the dream alive. May they keep the vision alive and may they never let it die. May they bring to birth that which they have conceived in Your presence.

May there be no abortions to the perfect will of God in their lives. We rebuke the devil and all of his emissaries. Father, come through for my sisters. I ask all this in the holy name of Your Son, Jesus.

Sisters, God will give you better than you asked. God will give you more exceeding abundantly above anything you can ask or think according to the power that is at work within you (Ephesians 3:20).

Now say this: I promise, Lord, I will not be defeated. I will encourage myself in You. I will wait on the promise, no matter how long it takes. I will be satisfied and content in the wait. I won't be lazy in the wait, but I will be about Your business. God, I trust in You. I will not lean to my own understanding, but in all my ways I will acknowledge You, because I know, Lord, You are directing my path.

Chapter 7
While You Are Waiting

I want to share with you some Scriptures the Lord gave me while I was waiting and trusting Him for a mate. I will also share with you a list of some books I feel will encourage you in your journey to wholeness, along with some proclamations and quotations that will boost your faith and minister hope to your spirit.

The first thing you must evaluate is your life, then maximize your personal potential. Everyone is born with creative gifts and talents from the Father. We owe it to God and to ourselves to maximize all that we are for excellence in service to His Kingdom. This is not simply a prerequisite for marriage, but for fullness as a whole person.

You are not one-half of some mystical whole that will only be created when you have a mate. You are to be whole when you meet that person. The miracle of marriage occurs when God takes two WHOLE individuals and makes them ONE.

Physically, take care of yourself. Make a balanced diet your lifestyle. Healthy eating is not simply a way to lose weight, it is to maximize your personal potential. Food is meant to be fuel, not fun. Eat less fats, less meat and eat more fruits, vegetables and grains. Exercise daily, not just your mouth, because we are good at exercising it.

If you can't afford a health club membership take walks, enjoy the sights of nature. Treat yourself to thirty minutes a day of healthy exercise. Let your mind breathe and your spirit relax. You'll feel better emotionally and your body will begin to tone up as you lose inches. If you can't go outside, walk in place, do a little jogging inside of your house. Do something.

Recently, I met a young lady in a wheelchair who is paralyzed from the waist down. She began to lift some small weights with her hands and do some upper body exercises. She lost many inches and over fifty pounds and she is paralyzed. What's our excuse?

Your body is the temple of the Holy Spirit and if you want to live a long and fruitful life for the Kingdom, possibly marry and bear children, the better shape your physical body is in, the better it will serve you.

Pamper yourself. Go get your nails manicured and have a pedicure. Get your hair done often. Try new styles. Save your money and go to a salon where they specialize in haircuts and styling. It may cost a little more, but they will fix your hair according to its texture and style it to compliment the shape of your face. Try a subtle color change or highlights to brighten you up.

Once every six months or so, try to get a massage. Sometimes you can find a day package at a salon-spa and have several things done for one price. You'll feel better about yourself and love yourself more. Take long bubble baths. Enjoy your femininity. Try a new style of clothes. Take a friend with you who will be honest and tell you the truth, wear something that is a little more flattering to your figure.

Buy some new earrings. Do something for yourself. Go out to a concert with friends if you don't have a boyfriend. Don't stay in the house. Buy your favorite CD, go see a good movie — something edifying. Enjoy your life. Love your life as a single person. Love your life right where you are or God can't give you another life. Say to yourself every day, "I love my life."

Stir up those talents and gifts you have. Work on your piano playing or take voice lessons. Improve on your talents and gifts. Learn how to be creative. Take an art class or learn a craft.

Mentally, stretch yourself. Watch the news. Know what is going on in the world. Contrary to popular belief, men like to have conversations with women. They like women who are able to intelligently converse. They are not all just looking at the outward package.

Read books. Find things in life that you enjoy doing. What are your interests and hobbies? I know a single young lady who was involved helping the deaf. She continued doing that after she married. She wasn't just an empty shell waiting for someone to come to her, she was out keeping busy and enlarging her personal borders. Enhance yourself mentally. Read books that challenge you, perhaps with words you have to look up in the dictionary.

Increase your vocabulary. Learn a new word or two every week. I have a friend who learned a new word every day for one year, thus adding to her vocabulary by 365 words. A man does want someone he can talk to.

Emotionally. Study yourself. Know your weaknesses when it comes to relationships. Deal with yourself in prayer with God. If you have been involved in codependent relationships, learn how to receive deliverance. Work on being emotionally whole and capable of having a good relationship with a man.

Stop being negative about everything. Become a positive person. Positive people attract positive people. When you are so sour, no one wants to be around you. Tell your face to smile. Soon it will radiate from your inward happiness rather than the direct order. Learn to laugh. Laugh at yourself. Increase your sense of humor. Men love women who laugh and enjoy life.

Most of all spiritually — get in touch with God. Work diligently on developing your first-love relationship. Pray the prayer David spoke, "Search me, O God, and know my heart: try me, and know my thoughts. See if there be any wicked way in me, and lead me in the way everlasting" (Psalm 139:23,24 KJV).

Make Jesus the Lover of your soul. Learn to know His voice and listen to what He is saying. Respond quickly in obedience. Deal with the root issues in your life and not with the symptoms. When the roots die, the symptoms will never return.

Pray God's will, not your will. Pray for your flesh to die and His Spirit to be alive in you. Learn how to deal with pain in your life and walk in victory.

I saw these words on a greeting card once and I loved them: "There are times in every life when we feel hurt or alone. But I believe that these times when we feel lost and all around us seems to be falling apart are really bridges of growth. We struggle and try to recapture the security of what was, but are lost in spite of ourselves. We emerge on the other side with a new understanding, a new awareness and a new strength. It is almost as though we must go through the pain and the struggle in order to grow and reach new heights" (Author Unknown).

When you are praying and discussing a mate with the Lord, pray the right things. Pray for a man with the character of God. There is a difference in a man of God and a man with the character of God. A lot of men who flow in the gifts of God are considered men of God, but they do not have His character.

Remember, you live with a person's character, not with their gifts. Their gifts are for the Body of Christ. At home you deal with the real person. Pray for a man who puts God first, his wife second, his children next before his ministry or job.

Pray to receive a thoughtful and unselfish man. Ask God to send you one who is able to share his inner thoughts. You want a man who truly loves his wife as Christ loved the Church and is willing to lay down his life for her.

I asked God for a MACHO man — a Man After Christ's Heart Only. I prayed for a discerning man who was sharing, caring, honest, sincere and generous. I longed for a flexible, dependable and patient man who was also humble.

Many women are praying about how much money he makes and they hope he is famous. Maybe he will make more money after you marry him and maybe he will become famous after you marry him. You can pray for looks if you want, but someone who is very good-looking and doesn't act good-looking becomes ugly very quickly.

Pray God's will. If you have a promise from God, you can take it to the bank. You can depend on it. Start expecting. Start believing that God is a God of His Word. He cannot lie. He will not go against His Word. Let His

Word dwell richly within you. Feed on the Word. Let the Word minister to your spirit. Let the Word heal you. It's a lamp unto your feet and a light unto your path. Hide it in your heart.

The following Scriptures are ones God gave me while I was waiting. Some of them I literally held on to for years. I still hold on to them for other promises God has given to me concerning my life and ministry.

> **Not one will lack her mate. For it is his mouth that has given the order, and his Spirit will gather them together. He allots their portions; his hand distributes them by measure. They will possess it forever and dwell there from generation to generation.**
>
> **Isaiah 34:16,17**

> **For the Lord God is a sun and shield; the Lord bestows favor and honor; no good thing does he withhold from those whose walk is blameless. O Lord Almighty, blessed is the man who trusts in you.**
>
> **Psalm 84:11,12**

> **Delight yourself in the Lord and he will give you the desires of your heart.**
>
> **Psalm 37:4**

> **The Lord will perfect that which concerneth me.**
>
> **Psalm 138:8 KJV**

> **Seek ye first the kingdom of God, and his righteousness; and all these things shall be added unto you.**
>
> **Matthew 6:33 KJV**

> **The righteous will flourish like a palm tree, they will grow like a cedar of Lebanon; planted in the house of the Lord, they will flourish in the courts of our God. They will still bear fruit in old age, they**

will stay fresh and green, proclaiming, "The Lord is upright; he is my Rock, and there is no wickedness in him."

Psalm 92:12-15

I hasten my word to perform it.

Jeremiah 1:12 KJV

Do not be afraid or discouraged because of this vast army. For the battle is not yours, but God's.

2 Chronicles 20:15b

None of my words will be delayed any longer; whatever I say will be fulfilled, declares the Sovereign Lord.

Ezekiel 12:28

What the righteous desire will be granted.

Proverbs 10:24

You will arise and have compassion on Zion, for it is time to show favor to her; the appointed time has come.

Psalm 102:13

Set your minds on things above, not on earthly things.

Colossians 3:2

Blessed is she that believed: for there shall be a performance of those things which were told her from the Lord.

Luke 1:45 KJV

"Do I bring to the moment of birth and not give delivery?" says the Lord. "Do I close up the womb when I bring to delivery?" says your God.

Isaiah 66:9

Make every effort to live in peace with all men and to be holy; without holiness no one will see the Lord.

Hebrews 12:14

God is not a man, that he should lie, nor a son of man, that he should change his mind. Does he speak and then not act? Does he promise and not fulfill? I have received a command to bless; he has blessed, and I cannot change it.

Numbers 23:19,20

I will give you the treasures of darkness, riches stored in secret places, so that you may know that I am the Lord, the God of Israel, who summons you by name.

Isaiah 45:3

Who carries out the words of his servants and fulfills the predictions of his messengers.

Isaiah 44:26

Therefore I tell you (speak your own name), whatever you ask for in prayer, believe that you have received it, and it will be yours.

Mark 11:24

Have faith in God. For verily I saw unto you, That whosoever shall say unto this mountain, Be thou removed, and be thou cast into the sea; and shall not doubt in [her] heart, but shall believe that those things which [she] saith shall come to pass; [she] shall have whatsoever [she] saith.

Mark 11:22,23 KJV

"The Lord bless you, my daughter," he replied. "This kindness is greater than that which you showed earlier: You have not run after the younger men, whether rich or poor. And now, my daughter, don't be afraid. I will do for you all you ask. All my fellow townsmen know that you are a woman of noble character."

Ruth 3:10,11

"For I know the plans I have for you," declares the Lord, "plans to prosper you and not to harm you, plans to give you hope and a future."

Jeremiah 29:11

The Lord is not slow in keeping his promise, as some understand slowness. He is patient with you.

2 Peter 3:9

All your words are true; all your righteous laws are eternal.

Psalm 119:160

He who is the Glory of Israel does not lie or change his mind; for he is not a man, that he should change his mind.

1 Samuel 15:29

But whoever listens to me will live in safety and be at ease, without fear of harm.

Proverbs 1:33

For God did not give us a spirit of timidity, but a spirit of power, of love and of self-discipline.

2 Timothy 1:7

And when you stand praying, if you hold anything against anyone, forgive him, so that your Father in heaven may forgive you your sins.

Mark 11:25

[She] is like a tree planted by streams of water, which yields its fruit in season and whose leaf does not wither. Whatever [she] does prospers.

Psalm 1:3

For if you possess these qualities (the fruit of the Holy Spirit in your human spirit) in increasing measure, they will keep you from being ineffective and unproductive in your knowledge of our Lord Jesus Christ.

2 Peter 1:8

In [her] heart a [woman] plans [her] course, but the Lord determines [her] steps.

Proverbs 16:9

You, O Lord, keep my lamp burning; my God turns my darkness into light.

Psalm 18:28

A righteous [woman] may have many troubles, but the Lord delivers [her] from them all.

Psalm 34:19

Everything is possible for [her] who believes.

Mark 9:23

For he has not despised or disdained the suffering of the afflicted one; he has not hidden his face from [her] but has listened to [her] cry for help.

Psalm 22:24

The Lord is good, a refuge in times of trouble. He cares for those who trust in him.

Nahum 1:7

Cast your cares on the Lord and he will sustain you; he will never let the righteous fall.

Psalm 55:22

A cheerful heart is good medicine, but a crushed spirit dries up the bones.

Proverbs 17:22

But godliness with contentment is great gain.

1 Timothy 6:6

There is surely a future hope for you, and your hope will not be cut off.

Proverbs 23:18

Be strong and take heart, all you who hope in the Lord.

Psalm 31:24

Now faith is being sure of what we hope for and certain of what we do not see.

Hebrews 11:1

Be on your guard; stand firm in the faith; be [women] of courage; be strong.

1 Corinthians 16:13

We live by faith, not by sight.

2 Corinthians 5:7

He remembers his covenant forever, the word he commanded, for a thousand generations.

Psalm 105:8

But when he, the Spirit of truth, comes, he will guide you into all truth. He will not speak on his own; he will speak only what he hears, and he will tell you what is yet to come.

John 16:13

And I will put my Spirit in you and move you to follow my decrees and be careful to keep my laws.

Ezekiel 36:27

For you have been my hope, O Sovereign Lord, my confidence since my youth.

Psalm 71:5

Why are you downcast, O my soul? Why so disturbed within me? Put your hope in God, for I will yet praise him, my Savior and my God.

Psalm 42:11

Share with God's people who are in need. Practice hospitality.

Romans 12:13

Humility and the fear of the Lord bring wealth and honor and life.

Proverbs 22:4

You hear, O Lord, the desire of the afflicted; you encourage them, and you listen to their cry.

Psalm 10:17

A [woman's] pride brings [her] low, but a [woman] of lowly spirit gains honor.

Proverbs 29:23

Yet I will rejoice in the Lord, I will be joyful in God my Savior.

Habakkuk 3:18

Those who sow in tears will reap with songs of joy. [She] who goes out weeping, carrying seed to sow, will return with songs of joy, carrying sheaves with [her].

Psalm 126:5,6

Surely then you will find delight in the Almighty and will lift up your face to God.

Job 22:26

Yet I am poor and needy; may the Lord think of me. You are my help and my deliverer; O my God, do not delay.

Psalm 40:17

Life will be brighter than noonday, and darkness will become like morning.

Job 11:17

Love must be sincere. Hate what is evil; cling to what is good. Be devoted to one another in brotherly love. Honor one another above yourselves.

Romans 12:9,10

The Lord your God is with you, he is mighty to save. He will take great delight in you, he will quiet you with his love, he will rejoice over you with singing.

Zephaniah 3:17

I love those who love me, and those who seek me find me.

Proverbs 8:17

He guides the humble in what is right and teaches them his way.

Psalm 25:9

Yet the Lord longs to be gracious to you; he rises to show you compassion. For the Lord is a God of justice. Blessed are all who wait for him!

Isaiah 30:18

See, I set before you today life and prosperity, death and destruction. For I command you today to love the Lord your God, to walk in his ways, and to keep his commands, decrees and laws; then you will live and increase, and the Lord your God will bless you in the land you are entering to possess.

Deuteronomy 30:15,16

If they obey and serve him, they will spend the rest of their days in prosperity and their years in contentment.

Job 36:11

Let us not become weary in doing good, for at the proper time we will reap a harvest if we do not give up.

Galatians 6:9

Let us hold unswervingly to the hope we profess, for he who promised is faithful.

Hebrews 10:23

Consider it pure joy, my [sisters], whenever you face trials of many kinds, because you know that the testing of your faith develops perseverance. Perseverance must finish its work so that you may be mature and complete, not lacking anything.

James 1:2-4

And the peace of God, which transcends all understanding, will guard your hearts and your minds in Christ Jesus.

Philippians 4:7

Now may the Lord of peace himself give you peace at all times and in every way.

2 Thessalonians 3:16

Peace I leave with you; my peace I give you. I do not give to you as the world gives. Do not let your hearts be troubled and do not be afraid.

John 14:27

This is the confidence we have in approaching God: that if we ask anything according to his will, he hears us. And if we know that he hears us — whatever we ask — we know that we have what we asked of him.

1 John 5:14,15

Before they call I will answer; while they are still speaking I will hear.

Isaiah 65:24

And receive from him anything we ask, because we obey his commands and do what pleases him.

1 John 3:22

Call to me and I will answer you and tell you great and unsearchable things you do not know.

Jeremiah 33:3

The Lord will keep you from all harm — he will watch over your life; the Lord will watch over your coming and going both now and forevermore.

Psalm 121:7,8

If you make the Most High your dwelling — even the Lord, who is my refuge — then no harm will befall you, no disaster will come near your tent.

Psalm 91:9,10

A good [woman] obtains favor from the Lord, but the Lord condemns a crafty [woman].

Proverbs 12:2

But seek first his kingdom and his righteousness, and all these things will be given to you as well.

Matthew 6:33

And without faith it is impossible to please God, because anyone who comes to him must believe that he exists and that he rewards those who earnestly seek him.

Hebrews 11:6

The Lord is good to those whose hope is in him, to the one who seeks him.

Lamentations 3:25

But if you will look to God and plead with the Almighty, if you are pure and upright, even now he will rouse himself on your behalf and restore you to your rightful place.

Job 8:5,6

Those who know your name will trust in you; for you, Lord, have never forsaken those who seek you.

Psalm 9:10

Those who belong to Christ Jesus have crucified the sinful nature with its passions and desires.

Galatians 5:24

It is God's will that you should be sanctified: that you should avoid sexual immorality.

1 Thessalonians 4:3

A wife of noble character who can find? She is worth far more than rubies.

Proverbs 31:10

The Lord will open the heavens, the storehouse of his bounty, to send rain on your land in season and to bless all the work of your hands. You will lend to many nations but will borrow from none. The Lord will make you the head, not the tail. If you pay attention to the commands of the Lord your God that I give you this day and carefully follow them, you will always be at the top, never at the bottom.

Deuteronomy 28:12,13

Those who trust in the Lord are like Mount Zion, which cannot be shaken but endures forever.

Psalm 125:1

To the [woman] who pleases him, God gives wisdom, knowledge and happiness.

Ecclesiastes 2:26

Surely you desire truth in the inner parts; you teach me wisdom in the inmost place.

Psalm 51:6

Do not let this Book of the Law depart from your mouth; meditate on it day and night, so that you may be careful to do everything written in it. Then you will be prosperous and successful.

Joshua 1:8

Therefore, get rid of all moral filth and the evil that is so prevalent and humbly accept the word planted in you, which can save you. Do not merely listen to the word, and so deceive yourselves. Do what it says. Anyone who listens to the word but does not do what it says is like a [woman] who looks at [her] face in a mirror and, after looking at [herself], goes away and immediately forgets what [she] looks like. But the [woman] who looks intently into the perfect law that gives freedom, and continues to do this, not forgetting what [she] has heard, but doing it — [she] will be blessed in what [she] does.

James 1:21-25

WAIT FOR THE LORD; BE STRONG AND TAKE HEART AND WAIT FOR THE LORD.

Psalm 27:14

Quips and Quotes
To Live By

◆

You can't build a reputation on what you are going to do.

◆

The best antidote to worry is action.

◆

Will anything change as a result of worrying about it?

◆

Face your fears with productive thought and behavior.

◆

Live one day at a time. Do not dwell on the past or worry about the future. Trust God and make the most of today's opportunities.

◆

Negative feelings can distort your perception of reality. When you pray, He will give you His peace and His perspective.

◆

Lord, when we are wrong, make us willing to change. And when we are right, make us easy to live with.

Lord, prepare me for what You are preparing for me.

◆

God is not looking for gifted people that He can make faithful. He is looking for faithful people He can equip to do anything He calls them to do.

◆

By the time I've finished minding my own business, it's time to go to bed.

◆

Feed your faith — starve your doubts.

◆

Once you love something, you have to let it go free. Once it is free, if it comes back to you, it's yours forever. If it doesn't — it never was.

◆

A woman's true character is revealed by what she does when no one is watching.

◆

Many women forget God all day and ask Him to remember them at night.

◆

If you look behind you — you'll get depressed.

If you look ahead — you'll get discouraged.

If you look up — you'll see God.

◆

The best way to forget your problems and your pains is to help someone else solve theirs.

God can heal a broken heart — but you have to give Him all the pieces.

◆

When life gives you lemons, make lemonade.

My Proclamation

I am what I think about all day long. I am going to practice telling myself the truth. According to Philippians 4:8, I will fix my thoughts on what is true and good and right. I will think about things that are pure and lovely in me as well as in others. I will think about all I have to praise God for.

I am filled with God's Spirit, wisdom, understanding and knowledge. He has given me ability and intelligence and has endowed me with all the skill, perception and knowledge necessary to do all I am supposed to do this day.

I have been given helpers with wise hearts who are full of understanding and skillful minds so that we together may carry out all God has planned for us this day.

I am able to do infinitely beyond — immeasurably more than anything I can ask or conceive, beyond all my hopes and dreams and more than I would ever dare to ask according to the power of God which does energize Himself within me this day. I will give God all glory for what will be accomplished through me.

I am uniquely, genetically and perfectly created for the task God has for me today. I was created by God who never made anything badly. His creation is wonderful, so I am wonderful. Divine perfection is within me. I love life. I love my life. I love people. I have ability. I can do things well. I am happy and grateful. I will treat myself with the respect due royalty, as I am a child of the King of kings.

I believe in me! In Him I live and move and have my being. I can make a difference in someone's life today. I have access to the power of God.

I am loved and worth loving and I love others. I am a gift from God to my friends and my friends are a gift to me. I enjoy people. It's a pleasure to do things for others. I do not fear being misunderstood because God understands me and knows what is best for me at all times. I will not waste a minute thinking about those who have done me wrong. I will practice instant forgiveness.

Nothing can happen to me that is too big for God to handle. I am not alone. No one can do anything to me without getting God's approval first. I am the apple of His eye.

I choose to forgive past and present hurts. I have given God permission to show me any hidden hurts and bitterness in my heart. I have committed my life to Jesus and believe that He is able to keep me. I am relaxing in Him.

I live in peace, joy, security and abundance. I will not worry about the future. My future is as bright as the promises of God. He will always provide for me. His will for my life is what I would choose for myself if I knew all that He knows.

I will not judge anyone for anything because Matthew says, Do not judge and criticize and condemn others, so that you may not be judged and criticized and condemned. For just as you judge and criticize and condemn others, you will be judged, criticized and con-demned (Matthew 7:1,2). Romans 2:1 says, "You, therefore, have no excuse, you who pass judgment on someone else, for at whatever point you judge the other, you are condemning yourself."

I realize the things that irritate me in others are a reflection of my owns sins; therefore, when someone annoys me I will look closely at myself to find the reflection, then I will quickly ask the Lord to forgive me.

My body is the temple of the Holy Spirit and is becoming the size and shape that pleases the inhab-bitant thereof. Therefore, I will see myself with the value that God places on me. I will follow the wisdom that Peter spoke of, to not be concerned about the outward beauty that depends on jewelry or beautiful clothes or hair arrangements. I will be beautiful inside, in my heart, with the lasting charm of a gentle and quiet spirit, which is so precious to God. This kind of deep beauty was seen in the saintly women of old who trusted God and fit in with their husband's plans (1 Peter 3:3-6).

I will interpret everything through the filter of the Holy Spirit. My words will be pleasing to Him and that which I say will bring life and hope to others. I want God's love to flow through me continually.

That which I desire most is going to happen. He fulfills the desires of those who reverence and trust Him. I will commit everything to the Lord. He will help me. I believe all God has promised me will come to pass. God does not lie. I praise Him now.

Author Unknown

My Prayer for You

Lord Jesus, I thank You today for being a great God. I praise You for being El Shaddai, the God who is more than enough. I thank You for Your faithfulness and for Your unconditional love poured out upon us.

Lord, today I come to You on behalf of my sister. I touch her with the grip of my faith and I intercede for her in Your name. I ask today that You touch her where she is hurting. I ask that You mend the hurts of the past and heal her from wounds that have pierced her soul through family, friends and relationships with men. I ask that she be made whole. Heal her so wholly that when she remembers the past, she will only think of the great healing that she has received from Your hand and no longer feel the pain.

May she carry the spirit of forgiveness in her life daily and learn to give instant forgiveness to all who wound her. I ask today that You help her deal with her pain and that You become her RELIEF.

Jesus, we look to You, the author and finisher of our faith. Jesus, there is no other that we can turn to during these times in our lives. Comfort my sister, minister Your peace to her and turn her mourning into joy.

Lord, You know the plans You have for her life. Help her to submit to Your will and to Your way and if she is not willing at this time, Lord, make her in the near future to be willing for Your will to be done in her and through her.

Lord, I pray that she will see herself as You see her and she will recognize the value that You have placed on her and that You have a great purpose and plan for her life. God, let her see how very special she is to You, and help her to love herself as You love her.

I bind deadly, negative emotions that try to attack her, and I command the enemy and all of his evil conspiracies against her to be cut off in the name of Jesus. I thank You that she was born and that You planned all the days of her life before the foundations of the world. God, may she rest in Your peace, knowing that all things are working together for her good and that in Your perfect timing, all other concerns will be perfected by You.

Father, I ask that You give her a burning desire for an intimate relationship with You and a hunger and thirst for Your Word and for the Spirit to dwell within her. I ask that You give her supernatural discernment to know what is of You and what is not of You. I bind the spirit of deception and I loose the spirit of truth in her life. I speak freedom from every spirit that would try to attach itself to her that is not like You.

May she wait on You and on Your perfect timing for her life. May she find joy in the wait. May she be strengthened by might in her inner being. May she mount up with wings as an eagle and may she walk and not faint. May she seek You with her whole heart and find You as the Lover of her soul.

May she become a worshipper of You and seek first Your Kingdom and all of Your righteousness, knowing that You will add all other things as You see fit.

Father, I thank You that when we pray to You, You hear us, and not only do You hear us, but You answer us. I praise You and magnify Your holy name. May she realize and know that You have not forgotten her, but You are working Your will out in her life as long as she remains obedient to You.

To the King eternal, immortal, invisible, the Almighty God, be honor and glory forever and ever. Amen.

Single woman, *you can wait just one more hour, because God has not forgotten you. I love you, and so does He!*

Recommended Reading

The Holy Bible

Telling Yourself the Truth by William Backus and Marie Chapian

Codependency No More by Melanie Beatty

Pursuit of Purpose by Myles Munroe

Understanding Your Potential by Myles Munroe

Releasing Your Potential by Myles Munroe

The Search for Significance by Robert S. McGee

Woman, Thou Art Loosed by T. D. Jakes

Every Single One of You by Carlton Pearson

All the Women of the Bible by Herbert Lockyer

As a Man Thinketh by Norman Vincent Peale

Love Is a Decision by Gary Smalley with John Trent

Love That Lasts a Lifetime by James Dobson

Please Don't Say You Need Me by Jan Silvious

Jesus Was a Single Adult by Bob and June Vetter

Famous Singles in the Bible by Brian L. Harbour

Love and Its Counterfeits by Barbara Cook

Single Woman — God has not forgotten you!!

About the Author

The ministry of Helen Stubblefield Trowbridge started as a young child. Coming from a home of godly parents, she was a miracle baby destined to follow in the footsteps of her missionary mother and pastor father.

Gifted in music and marked with leadership qualities, with the hand of God on her life, Helen attended Oral Roberts University and began to minister with an anointed group of young ministers, including Carlton Pearson.

After graduating from ORU, Helen began to minister with Evangelist Carlton Pearson full time and served at his side in many capacities over the years. Her faithfulness and the anointing qualified her to handle the varied duties she was given in every area of the ministry. She always says, "God is not looking for gifted people He can make faithful, but for faithful people that He can equip to do anything He calls them to do." She assisted him in founding the Higher Dimensions Ministry, the Higher Dimensions Evangelistic Center (now known as the Higher Dimensions Family Church), served on the Apostolic Council of Ruling Elders for the Azusa Fellowship and also ministered as the Associate Evangelist for several years, traveling on the ministry's behalf. She now serves on the Board of

Directors for Carman Ministries and also on the Board of Directors for Bridges International Ministries.

With the call of God evident on her life and an increased anointing upon her ministry, Helen was ordained by Higher Dimensions and served as the Pastor of Parish Relations, being responsible for the Pastoral Care and Missions Departments, along with various auxiliaries within the church. Still to this day, she has a burden for the local church and its purpose in the Kingdom and has been sought out by pastors to minister to their church staffs.

She and her husband Tim presently live in California where they have founded Trowbridge Ministries International, Inc. Helen spreads the spirit of unity in the Body of Christ, the heart cry of her ministry covering. Ministry has taken Helen around the world. Sought for a strong stand on holiness, she focuses on developing godly character in people's lives.

A powerful word with a prophetic anointing will minister to you as Helen imparts the truths of God's Word. Appreciated for her "realness," people are experiencing an added dimension of the presence of God through her ministry.